God Bless Amerika

A true life story filled with hardship, struggle, and tragedy but never without the presence of hope.

Its message will invigorate and strengthen your efforts with renewed resolve and confidence to face life's challenges in today's America.

By

Martin Agegian

© 2015 Martin Agegian

This work is inspired by true events, woven into a fictionalized narrative.

ISBN 978-0692435533

Dedicated to my father, whose life has always been a
precious inspiration to me,

and

to the millions of immigrants who reached for
America's welcoming hand and never let go.

Acknowledgements

Cindy Carter – who brought order out of the hundreds of scribbled, handwritten pages that defied understanding, other than, it had to be some sort of secret cipher gleaned from a newly discovered *Rosetta Stone*.

Jill Taylor – her grammar and punctuation skills kept the sentences flowing smoothly.

Cessy -- my wife, who by de facto became, on demand, a walking, talking dictionary with 99% accuracy – only God is perfect.

Mancy Gant II – his graphic designer's talents and computer skills created an excellent, meaningful, eye-catching cover.

Terri Geitgey – whose training and experience, framed by a gentle, patient, and understanding nature, guided this exuberant and excitable author's first book to completion.

My heartfelt appreciation and thanks to all.

Contents

Preface

It is this writer's wish that after you finish reading my father's story you will be energized with renewed purpose and hope towards achieving the goals you have set for yourself – but never forgetting that happiness and sorrow, success and failure, health and sickness are all part of life's panorama of unfolding events.

Remember, there are no short cuts or quick fixes, only the lessons learned from making good judgments and bad judgments.

Life is a precious, magnificent adventure that comes your way only once – give it your best shot!

Martin Agegian

Introduction

By the first quarter of the 20th century, over twenty million immigrants had reached America's welcoming shores. The promise of a bright new beginning beamed its ray of hope to these new Americans, least of which were the Armenians, who had come to escape the horrors of the 20th century's first recorded genocide.

In 1918, *Ambassador Morgenthau's Story* was published. In it, America's former ambassador to Turkey, Henry Morgenthau, wrote about the "race murder" of 1.5 million Armenians in the chapter aptly titled, "The Murder of a Nation".

How the world reacted to the Ottoman Government of Turkey's systematic liquidation of the Armenian people during the years between 1915-1919 will not be the focus of this narrative.

In 1914, the assassination of the Archduke Ferdinand of Austria and his wife by a young Serbian anarchist catapulted Europe headlong into the bloodiest war to date.

Europe became divided into two opposing sides—The Allies: England, France and Russia against the Central Powers: Germany, Austria-Hungary, and Turkey.

In 1915, the Ottoman Empire of Turkey encompassed most of today's Middle East countries.

Among the milieu of diverse races, peoples, and religions were almost three million Armenians who for several millennia had been living on their ancestral lands mostly in eastern Turkey.

Through the centuries, the fortunes of the Armenian Kings ebbed and flowed from dynasty to dynasty until eventually disappearing. What remained were the vestiges of a people whose fierce need for national identity kept their language, literature, music, traditions, and religion alive to this day.

Jesus' teachings came to Armenia by one of his twelve disciples, Bartholomew. In 301 AD, King Dertad decreed Christianity the religion of the kingdom, thus giving Armenia the unique distinction of being the world's first Christian nation.

Through the millennia, one dominant trait became ingrained in the Armenian national character—the ability to bear the terrible cost of mastering the art of survival by enduring the searing effects of pain, sorrow, and death—those fundamental requirements of life's syllabus for survival.

This fictionalized narrative, based on true events, is about a young Armenian boy tragically orphaned and filled with the haunting memories of terror and death. America extended her hand, he reached out and held tightly, never to let go.

1

Mariam

Kegham Agegian was born circa 1898 in a small rural village in eastern Turkey where Muslims and Christians had lived for years in segregated neighborhoods.

While in his early teens, Kegham's mother died during the birth of her third child, a girl. Her untimely death left behind a home filled with memories of a devoted wife and the lingering sounds of laughter, tender lullabies, and the gentle, warm embraces of a loving mother.

The full weight of family responsibilities immediately fell on young Kegham—finding a wet nurse for baby Victoria, preparing meals, and performing the never-ending household chores. Their father was one of the very few *giaours* (unbelievers) allowed to hold an important position in the government postal service. In the Turkish version of the American Pony Express, he delivered, fully armed, important classified government mail. Many times, his travels kept him away for days during which time the pain of loneliness intensified for the children.

One day, word came from an enterprising matchmaker that a childless widow was available in a nearby village.

His two boys, standing next to Victoria's crib, listened intently to their father's introduction to a thin, frail woman struggling to catch each breath. Alas, it was destined not to be. In a few months the poor woman left on her heavenly journey, a victim of an unknown malady.

Matchmakers doubled their efforts to find a healthier candidate for the beleaguered family. Before long Kegham, with Victoria cradled in his arms and ten-year-old Setrak leaning against his side, listened for a second time to their father's words of introduction.

The boys stared wide-eyed at the robust, looming figure of the second candidate. The light outside the open door barely filtered past her ample body that so generously filled the entrance of their home. What a far cry from that last lady—"What was her name?"

Mariam was hardly one bent towards shyness. She immediately greeted the boys with generous, powerful hugs that left little Setrak grimacing and gasping for air. Kegham respectfully maneuvered to protect his little sister from the next crushing embrace.

In the tumultuous weeks that followed, Mariam's warm and loving nature, propelled by an overwhelming personality, began to have its effect. Her talents seemed endless. She could read and write, a rarity amongst rural folks, especially women. The tender, lilting tones of a limitless repertory of songs filled every corner of their home. Meticulous with household tasks which Kegham happily relinquished.

Joy and contentment began filling the emptiness in their lives and the gap that often exists between children and stepmother never had a chance to develop. This energetic, rotund woman and her irresistible personality left little doubt that she had always been their mother.

"Thank you, dear Jesus, for guiding my footsteps to a wonderful husband and such sweet children. Amen"

"Oh God, please don't take our *'nor myreek* (new mother) from us. Amen"

2

First Born

In the Anatolian highlands of Eastern Turkey, April is a time of low scud clouds gently prodded by warm winds and sporadic rain showers.

For nearly a year, Turkish and Russian armies were at war venting each country's age-old enmity on the other.

Private Mustafa Karadeniz's imposing physical bearing and alert, penetrating eyes complemented by a high level of intelligence left little doubt that you were in the presence of a capable, dedicated soldier. His talents soon came to General Gurlu's attention. Before long, Master Sergeant Karadeniz was wearing the prestigious gold emblem of headquarter staff prominently ablaze on his black sheep's wool *kalpak* (cap). The badge gave the wearer special status making him responsible only to his general.

A weary, rain-soaked Mustafa entered his tent, lit the oil lamp, and with a long sigh slumped down on his cot. He had just returned after riding for over twenty hours in heavy rain delivering urgent dispatches to the front lines. The physical and mental strain had made inroads into his energy reserves.

The lamp's soft flickering glow sent its shadows dancing around the tent. Like a silent lullaby it was having its effect. Mustafa's eyelids started their downward journey in tandem with his chin which was soon resting on his coat collar.

First an isolated snore and then more at steady intervals flowed from the exhausted soldier. The lamp's undulating shadows and the steady sound of the rain beating against the tent were working their magic. Just as sweet oblivion was about to claim its victim, the tent's entrance flap abruptly opened.

Standing at attention before Mustafa's wide-eyed gaze was Corporal Mehmet. In a manner that ranged somewhere between official and theatrical, the corporal began: "Master Sergeant Mustafa Karadeniz, you are hereby ordered to report to General Gurlu – immediately – that is in all speed. That's an order."

The faint beginnings of an impish grin were being suppressed at the corners of the corporal's mouth from becoming a full blown smile. Mustafa was sure that this was one of Mehmet's comic acts that left the listener wondering if the message was authentic or a contrived nonsensical facsimile.

The urge to reprimand was building fast. "Corporal, I need to get to bed – now!"

Undeterred, the corporal continued, "Master Sergeant Mustafa Karadeniz, you are to report to General Gurlu…."

Mustafa started to think, "This fellow couldn't be so stupid to send me on a pretense." His anger was rapidly building to another level. "Mehmet, the whole camp is familiar with your concocted antics. I'm in no mood for your crazy games." Glaring, bloodshot eyes sent a clear message.

"This isn't one of my comic moments. May Allah strike me dead. I've been waiting all night. I have to admit I can't help myself. Maybe, someday after the war, I'll be one of Turkey's great comedians."

Mustafa rushed straight to the headquarter tent. "But why was that rascal Mehmet smiling?" Mustafa snapped to attention. "Reporting as ordered, Sir." The brief moment of silence accentuated the steady sound of the rain on the tent's roof. Two oil lamps, one hanging from the center pole and another on top of a rough wooden table strewn with maps, sent their competing beams into the dark corners of the tent.

The general's voice held a measure of excitement. "Mardiros Agegian, do you know him?" A bewildered Mustafa replied, "Yes, Sir. He's from my village."

The general continued, "He brought some very important news." A generous smile glowed across the general's countenance. "Mustafa, my boy, let me be the first to extend my heartfelt congratulations on the birth of your first child—a boy! As of now, you are on a six-day pass to go home."

Mustafa exerted herculean efforts to prevent a complete breakdown of his military bearing. Before he could respond, he was in a firm embrace and in a warm fatherly voice, the general continued, "Mustafa *yavroom* (dearest), there's no time to waste—off with you." This was the son the general had always wanted.

Mustafa's vocal chords struggled to respond. His general's words were so unexpected—so fatherly. "I...I... Sir I..." The general interrupted, "Hurry, my boy, make every minute count."

Indecision became the soul of agony. "Dare I shake the general's hand?" Too late, General Gurlu turned towards the table of maps. Mustafa snapped to attention, adding inches to his height, and with a parting salute that cut the air like a knife, about-faced and left.

The rain on his face helped to relieve the awkward moments inside the tent. No longer in the grip of fatigue, his energy surged as he headed for the stables.

His thoughts raced compounding one upon another, "A steady trot and I should be home in ten hours...eleven...no... at least by day break. Thank you, Mardiros, my dear friend."

Arslan's excited whinnies were music to Mustafa's ears as he approached the stables. "How I love that horse."

Two years earlier a lone horse grazing in a farmer's field had caught Mustafa's attention. Curiosity drew him closer. In seconds, their eyes locked on each other and in a moment that happens once in a lifetime, an invisible bond was forged between man and animal.

The farmer's voice droned on, "Look, perfect teeth…did you ever see such solid bone structure…here feel for yourself the power in these hind quarters." No response from the soldier. The farmer started to fret. Silence was a cause for worry. "He's having second thoughts. I'll adjust the price— Allah forbid he's found a defect." The silence continued….then Mustafa shouted out, "Arslan will be your name." The farmer disguised a sigh of relief and added his agreement, "Lion, a perfect name for such a gallant horse." The traditional handshake completed the sale.

As Mustafa adjusted the saddle straps, he caught out of the corner of his eye the smiling faces of his comrades in the adjoining stall. One prominent visage was Corporal Mehmet, now beaming a full smile.

Handshakes and embraces followed with words of congratulations. Mustafa mounted Arslan and turned towards the sentry gate.

One final, friendly jibe, "Mustafa pasha, don't lose another chance to visit home in nine months. That's an order," was the comic corporal's parting words. Mustafa waved to his friends as Arslan began a slow trot past the saluting sentry into the darkness.

3

Rifle Fire

Eleven hours since leaving camp; the rain was down to a fine, misty drizzle. For Mustafa, the sun was shining and joyous thoughts abounded. "Allah's greatest gift, a child born out of the loving union of a man and woman." Then, the most obvious thought cut through his happy musings. Mustafa shouted for the world to hear, "My family's name will live on!" Arslan added a whinnying response. "*Mash Allah –* you understood." Gentle pats caressed Arslan's neck while words of affection filled his ears.

The clouds were beginning to separate. The early morning rays of light began to filter through breaks in the overcast sky, bringing into view familiar landmarks. Home soon—a gentle nudge to Arslan's side picked up his gait.

The road began its gradual descent into the valley below. "There's the old stone shed." Mustafa's heart thumped a joyous beat, vibrating throughout his body. Excitement was affecting horse and rider.

The trot was about to become a full gallop when suddenly, from the dark recesses of a grove of trees, flashes of gunfire. The hissing sounds of bullets filled the air.

In an instant, Mustafa rolled out of the saddle onto the muddy ground—Luger drawn. Arslan moved a short distance away as trained.

More shots—mud and stone chips flew in all directions. Mustafa's voice boomed out, "Master Sergeant Karadeniz, First Army Headquarters." More bullets screeched by.

Mustafa tried again, "Master Sergeant Kara..." A voice from the thicket of trees cut him short, "Show yourself." Mustafa cautiously rose. Arslan immediately returned to his side.

Soldiers began filtering out from the shadows. Mustafa noted that their uniforms lacked military markings. The men also moved and conducted themselves in non-military ways. His observations intensified.

A young lieutenant came into view accompanied by two German officers. Nothing unusual--German officers were regularly assigned to Turkish units as instructors. The Turk was a fearless and tough fighter, but needed a dose of Prussian training and discipline if he was to fight in a modern war.

The lieutenant acknowledged Mustafa's salute while noting his gold headquarters' staff insignia. Mustafa continued to process everything unfolding before his eyes: "Misfits in uniform…not behaving like regular troops…."

The lieutenant interrupted Mustafa's thoughts. "Our apologies, Sergeant, for taking you for one of the band of Armenian infidels that attacked a military supply wagon a few days ago."

Mustafa noted the ploy. "First Army would have known immediately. What is he trying to hide?" Mustafa's curiosity picked up. The lieutenant turned to join the Germans. As he prepared to mount Arslan, one of the motley irregulars edged closer. Mustafa's towering figure looked down on a weasel-like misfit who couldn't wait to open the flood gates of a burning secret. The weasel snapped a quick glance back towards the lieutenant huddled in conversation with the Germans.

The flood gates opened. "Sergeant, we're going to Khunoos with orders to kill all the Armenian *giaours*." His grin widened. "Rape their women—bayonet the pregnant ones...you know, two for one." An evil grin exposed a mouth full of discolored, rotting teeth.

The lieutenant inadvertently closed the flood gates by feigning an afterthought. "Where did you say your destination was?" "Erzeroom, sir," replied Mustafa and turned Arslan towards the road.

Mustafa desperately fought to conceal the urgency that was consuming him. He held Arslan to a slow trot. In the distance, streaks of sunlight were reflecting off the roofs of his village.

Once out of sight and sound, Mustafa turned off the road in full gallop towards Mardiros' house while rapidly calculating, "They're beginning to mount and in less than ten minutes...." Mustafa's spurs dug deep into Arslan's sides as hooves churned up the soft, wet earth.

4

Horror and Death

Mardiros had just returned from his last mail delivery. Mariam waved as he led his horse to the barn. From a distance, Mustafa's cry, "Mardiros, Mardiros!" With arms waving, he raced towards the house. Mardiros eagerly waved back, happy that Mustafa was able to be home to celebrate the birth of his son.

Mardiros' smile quickly faded when Mustafa leaped off his horse. "Quick, Mardiros, there's no time—gather your family—hurry! We're going to my father's house." In the distance, the dealers in death were approaching at full gallop. The cold chill of imminent disaster gripped both men as they stood transfixed on the riders just minutes away.

Leaving was out of the question. Mustafa drew his Luger from its holster. Mardiros rushed towards the house, "Mariam! Mariam – quickly, to the barn." A confused, frightened Mariam, clutching Victoria to her breast with Setrak close to her side, rushed towards the barn.

In seconds they were buried under piles of hay. Mardiros' agonized pleading voice continued, "Mariam, keep the baby quiet—Setrak, not a sound son. Don't worry, Mustafa is with us." "Father" was the only word Kegham had time to utter. His father's strong hands pushed him into a niche in the wall hidden by a loose board. "Hold this board in place," were his father's last words. A bewildered Kegham, cramped in the niche, peered through a small knothole. His body started trembling.

Several horsemen slid to a stop. The weasel spotted Mustafa. Shots—Mustafa's chest burst open killing him instantly. Mardiros fired back, killing one of the misfits. A hail of bullets riddled his body as he staggered backwards through the open doorway falling against the wall panel hiding his son. The river of blood streaming from his body flowed towards the niche. In seconds Kegham's bare feet were standing in a pool of his father's blood. Terror began consuming his paralyzed body.

The weasel snatched Mustafa's *kalpak* (cap). A satisfied, sinister smile framed his discolored teeth. Another misfit futilely tried to subdue Arslan whose hooves wildly pounded the ground defying the pygmy's efforts to grasp the reins. "To hell with the beast. Let's find the rest of this infidel family," ordered the weasel.

In seconds, Mariam's pleading voice and baby Victoria's cries filled the barn. Two shots—silence and then Setrak's frantic sobbing voice, "Myreek— Myreek!" A rifle butt crushed his skull.

The weasel tried repeatedly to adjust Mustafa's kalpak but it didn't want to fit. "One less *giaour* family," sneered the weasel. An evil grin was embossed on his face. "Let's get to the next house."

Arslan stood motionless looking down at the still body of his beloved master. Several times his nose gently caressed Mustafa's face. A plaintive whinny seemed to say, "Oh, how I love that man."

5

Final Prayer

Father Nersess was eagerly looking forward to performing this first baptism since being ordained a celebrant priest two months earlier from Saint James Seminary in Jerusalem. He was going over a mental list of things necessary—pitcher of water, not too cold, holy muron oil.... In the midst of his preparations, for some unaccountable reason, the familiar image of an elderly, gentle priest drifted into his mind's eye. A short, stout man with bright, sparkling, clear eyes and a long, flowing, white beard cascading down his chest. Truly, a living example of one of the Old Testament's prophets.

Bishop Simonian never ceased to communicate a deep understanding to his students' needs. This tender-hearted teacher had very early recognized the sensitive nature of one special fourteen-year-old seminarian. The bishop's pleasant manner, like a loving parent, guided young Bedros for the next six years.

Bedros' journey to the priesthood could not have been entrusted to a more loving and dedicated teacher. It was Bishop Simonian's suggestion that Bedros take his priestly name after the 11th century Saint, Nersess Shnorali. So on the day of his ordination, the prostrate Bedros rose after the benediction and became Father Nersess.

"Oh, yes, I need to mark the passages in the liturgical text in their proper order...." The sound of gun shots outside abruptly stopped his preparations, and before he could react, the front door of the small church burst open. Two soldiers rushed towards a bewildered Father Nersess and dragged him outside throwing him before a gathering hostile mob.

Stones and obscenities began showering on the terrified young priest curled up like a ball with his arms tightly wrapped around his head, trying to ward off the barrage of stones. Blood flowed out between broken, crushed fingers. A large stone struck his mouth. Blood and bits of teeth streamed out of the gaping wound. His semi-conscious body was mercilessly dragged over to a crudely fashioned cross made from pieces of wood from the altar.

The grinning soldier's blood-stained hands impatiently struggled to rip the embroidered altar covering into strips, to tie the two sections to form a cross. Father Nersess' arms were spread and tied. Several plunges with a bayonet into the palms of the hand opened slits into which splinters of wood were driven.

The crucifixion was complete. The mob went into a frenzy. Jeers and taunts filled the air. "Where's your Jesus...Why hasn't he come to save you?!?" From a disfigured, bleeding mouth a faint prayer, "Jesus, my sweet Jesus...." A rifle butt crushed Father Nersess' temple mercifully ending his torment.

17

The killing and debauchery spread until every Armenian home was pillaged and every family destroyed. Like an epidemic, it ran its course. Now, it was time to collect the dead for the burial pits, which were hastily being prepared.

Turkish women swarmed into the Armenian homes like packs of wild dogs—snarling and fighting over furniture, rugs, and dinnerware; ripping gold earrings from corpses.

The work of these scavengers was as vicious and thorough as the marauding killers. Young children with handsome features were whisked away to be raised in Turkish homes, never to know their true identities.

So, on this bright sunny day in April 1915, destiny had ordained that one Turkish family and one Armenian family would leave behind a son to carry on their family name.

6

"We Do"

Dr. Robert Thompson, MD, had just finished the final week of internship at New York's Presbyterian Medical School Hospital. His gentle manners and caring ways were inexorably drawing him towards a small-town practice.

Joan Stanton, a recent graduate from Troy Teachers College, was actively seeking employment in a one-room country school. One Saturday night, destiny took charge and decided that Bob and Joan should meet during a church social in Troy, New York. The quiet, reserved doctor was soon overwhelmed by the vivacious, exuberant young teacher. Destiny went into overdrive setting the next stage in the lives of these two kindred souls.

After a few months of dating, it became increasingly clear that the doctor was losing the battle for bachelorhood and the teacher was fast falling into a serene surrender mode to the love of her life. It felt so natural to be together. Destiny continued its subtle machinations until the last "I do's" as doctor and teacher pledged to face life's challenges "till death do they part."

Destiny stepped in again as to the location of their honeymoon. The New York Diocese of the Presbyterian Church was considering reopening their mission in Khunoos, Turkey. Dr. Bob's name came to the board's attention and better yet, the doctor's wife was a school teacher.

The offer to run the mission was quickly accepted. A small town practice, albeit not in upstate New York, and a one-room school hardly in rural America—but then, who cares? It'll be one continuous honeymoon.

So, in the fall of 1912, the Thompsons, brimming with enthusiasm and deliriously in love, set sail for Turkey. "Now, what was the name of that place?"

7

Thompson Inc.

Three years later, the honeymoon express was still going at full throttle without a hint of slowing down. The medical division was busy setting fractures, preventing serious infections, assisting in difficult births and a host of medical problems that were relieved from the contents in the green box with the red cross on its cover.

The education division's one-room school was also thriving. At first, a few curious adults that soon gave way to a steady flow of children filling the classroom to capacity.

Joan's pointer touched each word on the blackboard. A mixed chorus of young voices chanted—"Good morning, dear teacher. How are you today?" A small boy answered, "My name is Aram." A little girl in the front row responded, "My name is Nazik." From the back row a shy boy spoke, "My name is Kegham."

8

The Honeymoon Ends

One summer evening, a few days before Bob and Joan were to leave for Turkey on their continuous honeymoon, friends invited them to hear a talk by Reverend Roberts on his fifteen years of missionary work in Turkey. For one and a half hours, the reverend spoke to a spell-bound audience about the eye-witness accounts of unimaginable atrocities that he and other missionaries had witnessed in 1895 against the Armenians.

Bob and Joan decided to pass up dessert. They thanked their friends, Rev. Roberts, and headed for the door. Outside, Bob took a deep breath. He caught telltale signs of anxiety coming over his lovely wife's naturally cheerful face.

"Joan, honey, that was in 1895, seventeen years ago." They walked to the street-car stop in silence.

Three years later, one sunny April morning their "continuous honeymoon" would come to a terrifying, abrupt end.

9

Searching for the Living

Gun shots shattered the early morning calm. Agonizing screams and pleading voices filled the air. Bob rushed out to the front porch of the mission.

A panorama of horror was unfolding a few hundred feet away. In a fleeting moment, the image of Reverend Roberts flashed by.

"Oh, God—Bob!" A horrified Joan clung to her husband's arm. They stood paralyzed as the unbelievable nightmare unfolded, shattering their senses.

The marauding jackals paid little attention to the two Americans standing like statues. There was nothing to hide. This was the will of Allah—"death to the Armenian infidels."

Terrifying, tangled thoughts rushed pell-mell through Bob's brain. His subconscious was trying to decide how to react to what his eyes were seeing and what his mind was processing. "Joan, honey, that was 1895, seventeen years ago." The refrain mocked his thoughts. Certain situations arise that are devoid the luxury of options—you are either a spectator or a participant.

Heart rending sights enveloped Bob and Joan as they hurried towards the Armenian homes, looking for any signs of life amongst the lifeless human carnage strewn in the streets.

"Bob, Bob!" The pleading tone of Joan's voice propelled Bob to her side. "Look! Oh, Bob, look! It's Nazik." Her anguished choking voice continued, "She's breathing!" Bob dropped to his knees and gently placed his hand under the child's blood soaked dress and lifted her away from the limp arm of a woman whose punctured body had bled all over little Nazik. "No doubt her mother," reasoned Bob. Nazik had been left for dead.

Bob, cradling the little girl in his arms, rushed past hateful eyes towards the mission. For the next horror-filled minutes, bodies became objects to rummage through for signs of life. Glaring eyes followed their every move.

Bob laid little Nazik on the bed and rushed back to Joan. She was standing amongst a cluster of mutilated bodies, her hands and dress covered with blood. Her face distorted and streaming with tears. "Bob, why—why?" "Please, honey, we've got to move as fast as possible," was all he could say.

Rickety carts with tell-tale squeaking wheels were busy collecting bodies, some still desperately clinging to life. A little boy with an abdominal wound was in convulsions. "He won't make it, Joan," Bob's voice was calm and final. It was impossible to continue.

Bob's thoughts were back at the mission and the three little girls already saved. "My God, look, there's Avedis!" Joan rushed towards the small boy whose left side had been pierced by a bayonet. Thanks to a rib, the thrust of the bayonet had been deflected. A quick appraisal saw a chance to save the child. Bob gently lifted the limp body. "Come on, Joan—I need to stop his bleeding. We've done all we can."

Joan abruptly turned her head as if she had just seen a long-lost friend. "It's Kegham!" A short distance away, her student was standing in the doorway with a dead man at his feet and a few feet away a dead Turkish soldier. A defiant horse with wild glaring eyes stood next to the soldier.

Kegham was mumbling incoherently, staring into space. Joan wrapped her arms in a tender embrace around her young student and slowly guided him down the bloody path towards the mission with Bob alongside cradling the silent limp body of Avedis.

The Stars and Stripes fluttering in the breeze left no doubt to all who had eyes its very clear message—"Don't think of doing harm to those under my protection." Old Glory's message kept in check the "wolf pack" trailing the Thompsons.

Once inside, Bob began his diagnosis by carefully and methodically checking Avedis' wound. Joan was busy attending to the needs of the terror-stricken girls.

Several stitches and the bleeding was brought under control. Avedis hadn't flinched once. Bob's eyes sent a message of respect and admiration for Avedis' tear filled eyes to see. "You're going to be just fine, son."

All the while, Kegham sat against the wall, watching. Bob made another diagnosis—"good, he's stopped staring into space...a positive sign...he's reaching for the real world. That a boy, Kegham."

Since early morning, unimaginable horrors had engulfed the lives of two young Americans. Their fortitude and steadfast efforts had been tested to the fullest and found not wanting by any measure.

"It felt so natural to be together." Now—where did we hear that before?

10

The Weasel's Poison Spreads

The weasel had cunningly spread his web of lies, so that when the body collectors came to a certain infidel's house, they would know the reason for the dead Turkish sergeant.

"Do you understand?" shrieked the weasel. "He was defending the infidel scum. That traitor even killed one of my comrades."

The retaliatory mood festered and began to build against the Karadeniz family. Mounting fear drove Mustafa's wife and baby to the mission. In a fearful, choking voice, she explained to Joan why a Turkish woman had to come to a Christian mission for help. Joan welcomed her in her limited Turkish and embraced the trembling young mother. Mustafa's parents had refused to leave their home.

11

Camp Comic No More

Arslan never left his beloved master's side. Every so often, his warm nostrils moved tenderly across Mustafa's face. Suddenly, Arslan reared up and galloped across the field and out of Khunoos.

Arslan's sweat-soaked body raced past the sentry post. General Gurlu was immediately informed. Arslan's wild, glaring eyes sent their own message. A frantic General Gurlu ordered Corporal Mehmet, with four of Mustafa's comrades, to go to Khunoos. The sight of the empty saddle assaulted his heart and mind with a fearful premonition of never seeing Mustafa alive again.

The troopers galloped out of camp with Arslan leading. They reached Khunoos in less than eight hours. Their horses, heaving chests covered with sweat, were on the verge of collapsing.

Mehmet leaped from his horse and stopped a cart piled with bodies. "What has happened here?" His anxious, high-pitched voice had little resemblance to that of the camp comic. One of the men began to relate the events of the last 26 hours.

"Around 50 soldiers rode into our village and headed straight to the Armenian neighborhoods where they began killing the infidels. One of our own, Hamid Karadeniz's son Mustafa—that traitor—defended an infidel family. He even killed one of our soldiers. We dumped his worthless carcass with the rest of the infidel scum," and then spat in disgust.

Before his expectoration hit the ground, Corporal Mehmet's hand had a firm hold of the old man's beard and in a stressed but controlled voice, he drew the wincing man closer. "Listen carefully. I want you to take me to Master Sergeant Karadeniz's body—now!" The sound of four cocked rifles added their own ominous meaning to Mehmet's words. The cart's squeaking wheels rolled on towards the pits with the troopers close behind.

One of the men remembered the approximate location of Mustafa's body. They found it covered with several mutilated bodies. The sight of Mustafa, his blood-soaked coat and bare feet, sent an avalanche of anguish and disbelief—it had to be a mistake! That was not Mustafa—it was someone else. A long agonizing pause followed.

Mehmet broke the silence, "No one is to touch him." Mustafa's comrades gently and carefully lifted him out of the pit. Mehmet, his eyes bulging with tears, continued, "Water!" A bucket of water appeared in moments. Gentle hands began cleaning Mustafa's face, hands, and feet. Then in a subdued voice, "his boots." There was no mistaking the consequences; the boots had better be found. In moments, trembling hands placed Mustafa's hastily cleaned boots at Mehmet's feet.

Mehmet thanked Bob and Joan for their kindness and escorted Mustafa's wife and child back to Mustafa's parents' home.

It was time to leave. Mustafa was returning to his military home. His father, weighted with grief, stood silent. Mother and wife wailed pitifully their last laments. Mustafa's comrades fought back tears. Only the barely audible sounds of sadness slipped through their pressed lips. One more thing had to be done. Mehmet barged into the mosque. An old *imam* faced the five troopers whose rage and anger-filled eyes only needed a spark to ignite.

Mehmet spoke to the *imam* in a way that left no doubt that not a word was to be taken lightly. "If any harm should come to the Karadeniz family or kin, the perpetrators will be hunted down like dogs and executed on the spot. By order of General Gurlu." Before the *imam* could respond, they left.

Mehmet placed Mustafa's boots firmly into the stirrups, carefully strapping his legs to the saddle. Next, the torso and head were held in place by boards placed beneath his army coat—dignity even in death, the final expression of respect from his comrades. Arslan, with his master in the saddle, proudly led the troopers out of Khunoos. Mustafa's head bobbed up and down, seeming to give an eerie approval.

The military funeral ceremonies left battle-hardened veterans in tears. General Gurlu, tormented with grief, watched the last shovelful of earth cover the grave. After the troops were dismissed, he remained, shoulders bent and head bowed down, staring at the mound of earth. "Hurry, my boy, make every moment count."

12

Survival DNA

By July, normalcy, like a fugitive, unabashed and unashamed, gradually crept back into Khunoos. Faint patches of green began carpeting the mass grave sites. The horrors of April would soon become another stretch of meadow land.

News of the genocide filled newspapers in America throughout 1915-1916. The US Ambassador, Henry Morgenthau, exerted his influence to assist religious and secular organizations to transport thousands of Armenians to orphanages and refugee centers in Egypt, Greece, France, Denmark, and the United States.

A late-night knock at the door. The glow from Bob's oil lamp revealed a cluster of pitiful, expressionless little faces. A Turkish farmer from a nearby village in hushed voice whispered, "Effendi, this is all we could save." Cart and horse disappeared into the late-night darkness; another heart had triumphed over indifference and fear.

Nazik, Avedis, Zabelle, and Arshalous were the first to leave. The girls clung to Joan, crying their little hearts out. Avedis' clear, calm words, "Thank you, Doctor Bob," burst the tear ducts, sending streams of bitter-sweet tears down Bob's face.

By June 1916, "Thompson Inc." had successfully helped send hundreds of Armenians to safe havens. Other equally dedicated missionaries of all denominations had saved the future of a people that had come to the brink of extinction. Refugees became immigrants—immigrants became citizens in countries all over the world.

The will to survive was definitely part of the Armenian peoples' DNA.

13

Happy Birthday

"Bob, I've decided to bake a birthday cake for Kegham. He has to be almost 18 years old. What do you think?"

"Well, I think...."

Joan's enthusiastic voice cut in, "Great, dear." Her sparkling personality had never lost its momentum since that fateful day at the church social. Joan continued, "I've decided that June 16 will be Kegham's official birthday—keep the oven at a constant temperature, dear." Bob chuckled to himself as he headed towards the clay oven. "Now, how do I do that without a temperature gauge?" Bright flames were building up the heat. "A few more pieces of wood should do the trick."

Joan looked over Kegham's shoulder. "Hmmmm." *The National Geographic.* Kegham was always engrossed with anything and everything to do with America. Indians, cowboys, the Wild West, National Parks, New York, Chicago, Detroit, forests of the Northwest, the Rockies, deserts of the Southwest, alligators of Florida—on and on, there was no end to the marvels of America from sea to shining sea.

A pan filled with cake batter was soon on its way to "master baker" Dr. Bob, who was exerting every ounce of intuition and guesswork to keep the elusive temperature in the clay oven "constant." In no time, the cake rose to the required height. "It had to be those last two pieces of wood," mused Bob.

The Thompson duet singing "Happy birthday, dear Kegham..." reached the ears of the curious outside the mission. "Those Americans. What is all that singing about?"

June 16, 1916, an 18-year-old Kegham faced Bob and Joan trying to show somehow the full measure of gratitude and love his heart could impart to the two precious people that destiny had brought into his life. "This is the happiest day of my life. It will never fade from my memory." Kegham paused. Bob and Joan looked at this young boy they had known for over four years.

"I want to say that I...." The full force of suppressed grief overcame Kegham. His voice lost the power to form words. He tried to catch his breath while fighting tears and uncontrolled sobs. Mariam's cries—gun shots—Setrak's pleading voice "*Myreek, Myreek.*" His father's lifeblood spilling out over the floor.

Joan quickly changed the direction of the moment—"Happy birthday, Kegham dear. Now don't forget, June 16 is your birthday." She gave him another hug and a kiss while Bob began extinguishing the lamps. The darkness inside welcomed the full moon's glow flooding through the mission's windows.

So much had happened in such a short time. Its impact would remain with them for the rest of their lives. But now it was time to sleep.

"*Keshare Pari, Kegham*"—"Good night, Joan"

"*Keshare Pari, Kegham*"—"Good night, Dr. Bob."

Kegham couldn't sleep—he had too much on his mind. He forgot when his thoughts faded and sleep crept in. "Tomorrow...tomorrow."

14

America Calls

Joan was about finished washing the supper dishes. Bob was at his desk re-reading a letter he was preparing to answer. Kegham cherishingly observed the two most important people in his life. Standing up, he focused his eyes on a point on the wall. An expression that belied feelings of regret and apology covered his face. Kegham struggled for the words he was sure would hurt the two people he owed so much and loved so dearly.

In a hesitant, barely audible voice, he began, "I want to go to Amerika." His eyes continued focusing on the wall. His words hadn't penetrated the consciousness of the others in the room. Bob was still reading and Joan was starting to dry the dishes,

It's a general rule that any second attempt will always be made with greater force. "I want to go to Amerika!" Bob looked up—Joan turned around. Reluctant to make eye contact, Kegham's eyes never left the wall.

"Of course, Kegham, we're all going back to America," was Bob's matter-of-fact reply. Kegham turned as Joan approached him.

Kegham continued, "You're the only family I have....I don't want to...."

Bob interrupted, "These are very dangerous times in Turkey. When we close the mission and make all the necessary arrangements with the embassy—then we'll all go home. It won't be long—just a few more months."

Determined, youthful impetuousness is a force that can overcome the most logical and reasonable argument. Bob and Joan made every effort to dissuade Kegham but to no avail. Months of waiting had no appeal—only one option—America now!

An energized and confident young man began to explain his plan in detail. "I'll reach the port of Trabzon on the Black Sea in five days. Find a ship going to America and work my way...etc." Bob and Joan listened without responding. Waiting for something they didn't know what. Kegham ended his detailed explanation with "It's that simple."

For the next several days, the Thompsons' strategy was to wait. Time would weaken Kegham's impulsive decision in their favor. Kegham felt time was on his side. Bob and Joan would see things his way. America was calling. Kegham couldn't wait to answer her call. Heavily weighted, anxious days dragged by—the Thompsons lost. Bob reluctantly composed an impressive, two-page "To Whom It May Concern" letter stating Kegham's health, character, and the tragic circumstances about his family.

It was very impressive with the diocesan seal and official signature: Dr. Robert Thompson, MD,

Director. Joan added a US ten-dollar bill in the envelope with Bob's letter, plus a few Turkish liras.

America was calling and another immigrant eagerly answered—"I'm coming AMERIKA." Apples, cheese, and bread wrapped in paper tucked inside his jacket was more than most immigrants had starting their journey to the "land of plenty."

The three members of "Thompson Inc." stood motionless for what seemed like eternity. Kegham was drawn into the arms of these fantastic "honeymooners." They cried, hugged, and hugged again. "Keep my parents' address in a safe place," reminded a tearful Joan. Dr. Bob could barely muster a smile that seemed so out of place on his saddened face.

The only heir of one Armenian family was about to begin an odyssey that would change his life forever. The only heir of one Turkish family was to grow up cherishing a father he would never know.

15

Destiny

Kegham reached the port of Trabzon late afternoon of the fifth day. So far on schedule, in fact, just as he had planned. It boosted his confidence to another level.

Several freighters were anchored a few hundred feet off shore and another was unloading cargo dockside. Hereafter, all decisions were going to be subject to careful analysis plus a hefty dose of intuition.

The impact of an unexpected dilemma; finding a ship going to America. It wasn't going to be so simple. Darkness was gradually enveloping the harbor. The dim glow from several oil lamps highlighted the shadowy forms of longshoremen unloading cargo. Some words in German from the deck of the freighter drifted into the night air.

A solid overcast sky hid the moon's glow. Darkness became an important ally. Crouched under the pier, Kegham waited for the next phase of his plan to show itself. The stevedores finished for the night and started to leave. From somewhere on board, a phonograph needle sent the scratching sounds of a waltz into the night. A bit of the Fatherland for homesick seamen. A few more records and then only the rhythmic measured sounds of waves ebbing and flowing upon the shore.

Kegham, his knees drawn up to his chest, stared at the shadowy outline of the nearest ship a few hundred feet away. He was sure he could get to the ship even though he had never learned to swim!

He began instinctively dog-paddling towards the freighter. He made sure his cap was pulled tight around his head. Bob's letter and the ten dollars had to stay dry.

As he neared the freighter, the hull's steel plates loomed up above his head. The ship's Jacob's ladder was up for the night. Nothing to cling to and no one in sight! A severe bout of anxiety started rapidly growing. Panic was beginning to invade his body. "I should have listened. So stupid, so ungrateful." Tight muscles thrashed the water. "Help—Help— Help me!"

A face appeared at a porthole and quickly disappeared. From the deck several seamen talked excitedly in an unfamiliar tongue pointing at Kegham in the dark waters below.

Kegham went under several times. The Jacob's ladder dropped down and in seconds desperate hands grasped the bottom rung. Shivering and dripping wet, Kegham stood facing several curious seamen. "I'm Armenian. I want to go to Amerika." The words flowed, pleading, begging and crying; desperation in full bloom. The unbridled confidence five days earlier was rapidly unraveling.

An officer appeared in an immaculate white uniform and spoke in excellent English, "I am Lieutenant Hernandez. What were you doing in the water?" The officer was born in Fresno, California. At 16 years of age his parents had moved back to Argentina.

The crewmen's bewilderment changed to an intense interest in the dripping wet young man clutching his cap. Inaudible words punctuated with half-finished sentences, Kegham began relating what was hidden deep inside his soul. Hernandez listened holding back any reaction. The crew stood waiting for more words from this late night visitor aboard the *Patagonia*.

"We were in New York last year. I read about the plight of the Armenians." The First Officer's eye caught sight of the Captain on the bridge. He turned and saluted and began explaining the reason for the commotion. The Captain listened, spoke a few words, turned and disappeared into the darkened bridge.

Luis Hernandez turned towards Kegham who had all the appearances of a condemned man seconds before the trap door opened. A broad smile lit up the First Officer's face, "The Captain has allowed you to remain on board. We're scheduled to leave early tomorrow morning. First stop is the Azores and then Buenos Aires."

"Reprieve!" The trap door never opened. Lieutenant Hernandez issued orders to the crew and left.

Kegham was led to a small cabin. A clean white blanket, several large towels and dry clothing hung from hooks. The parting crewman's cheerful smile spoke clearly, "Welcome aboard the *Patagonia*, Amigo."

Kegham hung his wet clothes on the several hooks lining the wall. The money and Dr. Bob's letter had survived the panic-stricken moments in the water. He had done a thorough job with oil cloth and candle wax. Not a drop of water had reached its contents.

Kegham sank into the hammock, pulled the blanket over his exhausted body, and fixed his eyes on the ceiling. The stressful journey and especially the last hour had claimed the last pockets of consciousness. Submission was the only course. Each breath drew him farther away from the uncertainties of the moment and deeper into the secure world of dreams.

Amerika — Amerika — Amer —— A...

16

Unexpected Delay

The *Patagonia* slipped through the Straits of Dardanelles. Constantinople was close enough to see people in the streets. It would be the closest he would ever again come to Turkish soil.

Kegham's eyes scanned the deck. Crewmen beamed friendly smiles. He had to reassure himself that what was happening was real. A sense of deep relief and accomplishment filled his thoughts.

By the second day, the *Patagonia* steamed by myriads of Greek islands dotting the clear blue waters of the Mediterranean. Clusters of whitewashed houses, perched on hilltops like gleaming opals, reflected the sun's rays.

Kegham joined the crew in their shipboard duties, scrubbing, scraping, cleaning, painting, polishing, etc. The crew spoke in Spanish and Kegham in English. Yet communication was made with head movements, hand gestures, and facial expressions. It was amazing the communication that was made without words.

All ships were being carefully scrutinized by the British Royal Navy and the German Imperial Navy who checked their manuals for tonnage, class, markings, and configuration. The Argentine flag was rarely seen in these waters. It possessed no threat to either of the belligerents. The *Patagonia* continued on its course.

The Rock of Gibraltar was so close that Kegham could see the indigenous monkeys sunning themselves. Then into the wide Atlantic—next stop the Azores.

A few days out, Kegham came down with a fever and was confined to his cabin. They reached the Azores none too soon. The Portuguese doctor made a routine diagnosis—not serious or contagious but Kegham required observation and rest.

The *Patagonia* was scheduled to depart that evening, so it was adios. Kegham slowly made his way down the ladder carrying a box of gifts from the crew. He waved and the crew waved back their farewells. Lt. Hernandez lent some humor, "Safe journey, amigo. Many American ships stop here—don't swim; use a boat the next time." The Captain was watching from the bridge and flashed a quick smile.

A week of rest and care and in no time Kegham was up and about. Second helpings of food brought his energy level back. The hospital staff provided the pleasant young man with underwear, a two-piece suit, shoes, shirt, and a bright red tie. "The American immigration officer will wonder if this fellow was a bona fide immigrant or a tourist who had wandered into the wrong line." The doctor's comment brought

45

a chorus of laughter and hugs and kisses from all directions. Kegham thanked everyone.

Soon, word came that the freighter, *Roma*, had just docked in the harbor. Captain Gillespie didn't need convincing about his new passenger's need to get to America. Kegham was welcomed aboard, no ticket, no questions asked—the *Roma* was full of immigrants. The cowboys, the Indians, yes, even the alligators were all waiting. Next stop—America!

17

Kindness Abounds

Miss Liberty was nowhere in sight as two tugs escorted the *Roma* towards the docks at Newport News, Virginia. The awestruck new Americans leaned over the rails, straining their eyes, spellbound, devouring everything in sight. Kegham's heart thumped beneath his suit, shirt, red tie, right down to his new underwear. It felt like being reborn. America had opened her doors "to the huddled masses." Her welcome mat would never wear out.

Kegham's ability to speak English helped to speed him through Customs and Immigration. "Health status—Excellent. Date of birth—June 16, 1898 (Thanks, Joan!). Born in Khunoos, Turkey. Armenian extraction, names of living relatives—mother, father, siblings, etc. The questions about family burst like a time bomb, unmercifully without warning.

Kegham started stammering, trying to answer the questions about family members. His response was lost in a sea of tears and short gasps of breath. The examining officer didn't know how to react and waived for another officer. Now, there were two confused immigration officials. Kegham's trembling hands searched inside his coat for Dr. Bob's oil cloth packet.

After reading the contents, the officer had his answer. He carefully folded the packet's contents and returned it to Kegham. "Welcome to America, young man." It was July 26, 1916.

Past the stile gate and in a few steps, Kegham was on the sidewalk. He didn't move for a while as the other immigrants filed by. A short distance away, he came to a beautifully manicured park. Huge chestnut trees spread their shade over benches filled with people reading, talking, resting. It was so peaceful, so clean and orderly. He found an empty bench and spent the next hour observing children frolicking on swings and slides. In the street, horse-drawn wagons were competing with the automobile.

Joan had told Kegham to go to Watertown, Massachusetts, where the Armenian community was well established since the 1880's. A few inquiries and he was soon standing at the ticket window of the train station.

"I want a ticket for Watertown, Massachusetts." He pushed his ten-dollar bill through the opening and waited. He got back two tickets and $4.25 in change. Kegham's accented English and blank look indicated to the ticket master that he needed help. "When you get to New York, do not leave the train. In about an hour it will leave for Boston. Get off the train at Boston and go to track number 8, where you'll board train number 14. It leaves at eleven a.m. and arrives in Watertown at twelve noon."

The intense concentration on Kegham's face meant that there were still some gaps in his understanding and a little additional clarification might be in order. The patient ticket master started again. After the second attempt, Kegham smiled, "I understand. Thank you very much, sir."

"You are quite welcome, young man."

Kegham wondered how those immigrants who couldn't speak English got through the questioning. "Kegham, dear, this is America. There are interpreters ready to help those unable to communicate in English."

Kegham headed for track 11. The big clock over the archway was approaching 3:00 P.M. Three hours wait before boarding. About 6:00 P.M. passengers began gathering at track 11. Kegham made a mental note of the kind and helpful Americans he had met so far. "Were they all like Bob and Joan?"

From the gathering crowd, the sounds of Armenian being spoken alerted Kegham. "Yes, from those two boys over there." Kegham rushed over— "Yes, Hye am" (I'm Armenian). Two teenage brothers, Hagop and Zaven Margosian were from Mardin, Turkey. They had lost all eight members of their family. Their escape through the Syrian Desert followed to the letter the syllabus for survival. Beatings, deprivation, hunger, and inhospitable villagers were at every turn. They followed a camel caravan for weeks begging for food and water, feeding camels, pitching tents with plenty of spontaneous

49

beatings for payment and always scavenging for scraps of food.

Kegham listened. His admiration for the two brothers knew no bounds. Interspersed between the brothers' story of survival, Kegham's thoughts were crowded with Dr. Bob and Joan--clean beds, love and kindness, a big soft hammock, smiling seamen, Lieutenant Hernandez, the wonderful medical staff, new clothes, shoes...

By the time they were in their seats, the boys were friends for life. In New York, they shook hands, embraced and parted. The train pulled out of Grand Central Station exactly on time.

The sixty-minute layover in New York was just enough time for new passengers to board. The train started its slow departure out of the station. The joy meter was fast approaching maximum.

Tall buildings, filled with lights, passed by. The impact was hypnotizing. The cushioned seat and dimmed lights all conspired to weaken the resistance to stay awake. Kegham was soon wandering in and out of slumber's twilight zone. The excitement of America was continually energizing him. The past still had a firm hold on his thoughts. He needed more time. Nothing abides; all things flow; nothing remains constant. The future is constantly unfolding while the past is being filed away in memory's archives.

18

349 Elm Street

The transfer in Boston to the Watertown train was handled like he had done it a hundred times. Kegham walked out of the Watertown station exactly at noon. From Khunoos to Watertown in little over a month. It wasn't a dream but it sure felt like one.

"Armenian Church—yes. See that streetcar stop up the street? Catch the No. 8 and get off at the 4th Street stop. You'll be at 4th and Johnson. Walk a few blocks up Johnson. You can't miss it—I think it's called Saint Gregory."

"Thank you, sir."

The hexagonal cupola has been an architectural feature of Armenian churches since the 5th century. It stood out like a beacon. Quick steps, not quite running, he reached the church.

All immigrants have identical needs—their heritage, culture, and religion to sustain them especially in new and unfamiliar surroundings. Association with compatriots is vital and nourishing.

Father Levon was in the rectory that very moment. He quickly sized up Kegham. Just the type of priest a newly arrived immigrant needed. "Come Kegham, follow me." Kegham trailed the spry priest out of the church side door. Father Levon, ever alert, held back further talk. Kegham's eyes and mind were occupied with the sights. The paved streets were lined with homes and all surrounded with neatly trimmed lawns. Old elm trees lined both sides of the street. To Kegham, it was the closest thing to paradise on earth.

They came to a small house partially hidden behind a shoe repair store. Kegham followed the priest's black flowing cassock up to the front door. Father Levon knocked once and opened the door. "Rose—doones?" The response came back, "Aye yo!"

A heavy-set woman in her late forties appeared at the door. A cheerful voice and penetrating smile radiated straight towards Kegham. "My God… Mariam!" A deep yearning gripped Kegham.

They entered the tidy little house. Father Levon introduced Kegham. Rose hugged him in a warm, powerful embrace. "Oh, Mariam—Myreek!"

"Welcome to Watertown, my dear."

Father Levon continued, "Do you think Kegham could—that extra room—maybe he—

"Yes," was Rose's quick reply.

"Good, that's settled," replied Father Levon, with a relieved sense of accomplishment.

The trio sat at the kitchen table and for the next half hour drank tea and ate freshly baked *kata*. It wasn't long before George, Rose's older brother, popped in from the store to see to whom the new voice belonged. George was just as excited as his sister to meet the new boarder. "Welcome to America and welcome to our home!" He offered a firm, friendly hand shake. "I think I heard the store door." George excused himself and rushed back to his shop.

Father Levon also decided to head back to church but not before a bag full of *kata* was tucked under his arm. *"Shunoragal am"* (thank you). He left with visions of hot tea and *kata* before bedtime. If visions of *kata* weren't exactly dancing, they were certainly leaping.

Rose hummed a tune as she carefully placed a third plate on the small kitchen table. She paused for a moment. An excited happy glow radiated from her face.

Kegham was told in no uncertain terms to just sit. She didn't need any help. Rose's glow intensified. All the years, only she and George were present at dinner time, and now—she gave a quick glance from the corner of her eye at Kegham who responded with a warm, appreciative smile.

In 1882, George, 16, Rose, 14, and their parents came to America—first to Boston and then to Watertown. Their father was tragically killed in an accident at the Hood Rubber Plant. Their dear grieving mother's broken heart never healed. In a few years, she too left to join her husband.

In the years that followed, the bonds between brother and sister grew, fostering a dependence on each other. George went on to learn shoe repairing and opened his own store. The small house behind the store fit perfectly into their plans.

The years slipped by and neither had married. The shoe repair business earned enough for both. It wasn't long before George made the last payment on the mortgage.

Rose spent a great portion of her time in church-related work. But now! A most welcomed disruption in the entrenched routine of their lives.

In no time, Kegham became a part of the Armenian community. Playing Tavloo (backgammon) in the coffeehouses, discussing world affairs—the focus always on the turmoil in Turkey.

He couldn't wait to return to the little house on Elm Street to discuss with Rose and George the events of the day. Rose listened and watched Kegham. Her heart was beginning to beat the rhythm of a mother's love.

One day, a customer mentioned to George that Hood Rubber was hiring part time help. Monday through Friday, from 8 p.m. to 11 p.m., at $.50 per hour.

Early the next morning, Kegham sprinted the two miles to the plant. Between the huffs and puffs, he calculated $.50 x 3 = $1.50 x 5 = $7.50 per week.

"Run faster, Kegham, before someone else gets the job!"

A jubilant, perspiring Kegham rushed past George, "I got the job!" and without pausing headed for the store's back door.

"Rose is at the church!" shouted George. A quick 180-degree turn—full speed to St. Gregory's. Father Levon, Rose, and Kegham celebrated the good news in front of the altar.

The little house at 349 Elm Street was bursting with the sounds of merriment during and after dinner. By 1:00 a.m., common sense prevailed. Kegham lay in bed looking up at the ceiling, reviewing the exciting events of the day. "What's today—Thursday—no, Friday—yes, Thursday—$7.50 per week. Report to work on Monday at 7—no, 8 p.m.—no, 7:30 p.m. $7.50 x 52…" Sleep was coming on fast. "God bless Amerika."

19

Dear Son

Kegham was fast becoming a part of the family. The impact he was making on the lives of Rose and George was growing exponentially. It was like an invisible strand entwining the hearts of brother and sister. 349 Elm Street was fast becoming home to the young boarder.

Delightful news: Kegham would start full time, 50 hours a week plus a modest pay raise. The multiplying began in earnest. Kegham was well on his way to becoming Watertown's first Armenian "millionaire."

The matter of rent had always been on Kegham's mind. Each time he broached the question, Rose found a way to put it off, but the budding "millionaire" refused to be side-tracked.

Kegham's strategy was to threaten to leave unless he paid rent. Rent was never an issue for Rose or George. The cultural barrier against a family member paying rent complicated the delicate situation.

Reluctantly, Rose conceded to Kegham's terms; thirty dollars a month for room and board with a proviso that once a week, Saturday or Sunday, they had dinner at Arsen's Armenian restaurant courtesy of Kegham. "Sign, Rosie," urged George, "before our

Kegham decides to pay the electric, gas, and water bills." This brought down the house.

Rose was determined not to accept rent. In a few days she found the way. George slapped his knee, "Sister, you're a genius!" As Kegham proudly paid his first month's rent, George and Rose smiled at each other like two Cheshire cats. By noon, Rose had deposited the rent money in a savings account in Kegham's name.

20

First Christmas and New Year

Kegham's first American Christmas was a wonderful series of revelations. The live Christmas tree in the parlor with real candles burning precariously on the ends of the branches while the fire department was on ready-alert, their stallions fully harnessed all through the holiday season. Santa Claus in all his regalia, a blanket of snow, and carolers completed the picture.

The holiday season began with Thanksgiving and continued through December 31st, New Year's Eve. *"Shunaravor Nor Daree* (Happy New Year), Kegham." Rose tenderly kissed Kegham, reluctantly releasing her strong embrace. George in turn hugged Kegham but had to turn away as calloused hands wiped away a few bulging tears. Kegham excused himself and went to his room. It had become an emotional experience for everyone.

Brother and sister sat facing each other around the kitchen table as they had done for so many years, but tonight it was different. A few feet away was the light of their eyes.

Kegham looked up at the ceiling. Thoughts of joy and contentment reflected off the ceiling. 349 Elm Street was home, and Rose and George were becoming like—he wasn't quite ready to say—mother and father.

The ceiling faded and in an instant, he slipped into a deep sleep.

It should have been done sooner, but the journey from Khunoos to Watertown had crowded out everything. Now, it was time to write Dr. Bob and Joan about his fantastic journey and all the wonderful people who had made it possible. He composed a long, detailed letter, sealed it and proudly wrote the return address, 349 Elm Street, Watertown, Massachusetts, USA.

21

The Stantons

Joan's parents could barely contain themselves when Kegham introduced himself. Their questions were endless. They attentively listened as their young visitor explained the work at the mission. Outward signs of pride and love flowed from both parents.

Kegham didn't mention the dark side of the horrors of April. He didn't know how. He didn't want to. He wasn't prepared to talk on the subject. It was best left unsaid.

Joan's parents expressed concern that it took months for a letter to get to Turkey and just as long to get an answer back. Since 1912, they had received only 10 letters. The war made correspondence even more difficult. Kegham gave Mrs. Stanton his letter to go with their next letter to Bob and Joan.

That evening, during dinner, Kegham couldn't help silently contemplating the enormity of the dining room. It was at least twice the size of Rose's kitchen and pantry combined. He felt isolated sitting at the end of the massive table. A beautiful oriental rug lay under his feet and oil paintings lined the walls. Elegance abounded throughout the house. The Stantons were a dignified and cultured family.

Mrs. Stanton insisted that Kegham stay over Saturday night. The giant four-poster bed was almost as big as his bedroom back home. That night he scanned the ceiling but nothing happened. He turned over on his side and was soon asleep.

Sunday morning, Kegham was served a full-fledged American breakfast: eggs, bacon, waffles, maple syrup, toast, jam, and coffee. Too bad they weren't aware of Rose's *kata*.

The moment had come to leave with just enough time to catch the last train for Watertown. Mrs. Stanton hugged and thanked Kegham for all the first hand news about their Joan. Mr. Stanton seconded his wife's remarks with a warm smile and handshake.

Outside, an exciting first waited; an automobile ride to the station. "Someday, I'll own one just like this," thought Kegham.

George wasn't sure which train Kegham would be on so he came early enough for both trains. Three and a half hours later, Kegham hugged a happy George and they headed for the streetcar stop.

The moment Kegham entered the house, it was just as if a switch had been tripped. The house came alive. Joyful voices rebounded off the walls. The table was already set and waiting. Enticing odors seeped from the cooking pots and in the oven, *kata* was warming up.

After the bone crushing hug, ala Rose, and a kiss that left its mark for almost a full minute, the

61

occupants of 349 Elm Street were in their chairs around the small, round oak kitchen table. Between bites of *kata*, he looked at George and Rose with an orphan's yearning for parents creeping into his inner most thoughts. "It's only eight o'clock, folks. I'm going over to Varham's house for a while." Varham was a senior at Watertown High. Even though Kegham was not much older, he acted and felt older in so many ways. The burdens of sorrowful childhood memories age a child's heart, paving the way for early maturity. Varham, or for that matter anyone else, would never know the painful secrets locked deep inside Kegham.

"Kegham *hokees* (dearest), how was your visit?"

"Varham's mother sends her regards," answered Kegham and continuing, "Rose, no one can bake *kata* like you." Rose shot out of her chair. George directed a quick wink towards Kegham as they rushed for their chairs. In no time, laughter and happy voices filled the small kitchen at 349 Elm Street.

It was getting late. George was already in bed. Tomorrow would be another day ripping off worn soles and heels. Kegham kissed Rose and went to his room.

Alone, deep in her thoughts, Rose sat with her elbows on the table—her hands cradling her chin; she stared at the cups, dishes, and the few scattered crumbs on the table. "Dear God, thank you for bringing *anoushik* (sweet) Kegham into our lives."

In bed, Kegham remembered the embroidered words "Home Sweet Home" set in a picture frame at the Stanton home. The inner glow of joy filled his room. He was home. Sleep came instantaneously.

22

The "Honeymooners" Return

The long-awaited letter arrived just a few days after the Stantons had mailed theirs. The letter opener lost out as eager fingers tore the envelope open. "Bill! Bill! The children are coming home!" Her husband came charging from the day room leaving a trail of wrinkled Oriental rugs in his wake, almost slipping on a stretch of polished floor.

Edith reread the letter while Bill studied the postmark. The exuberant and jubilant parents started calculating. "I wonder if there's a train station in Khunoos." Sorry folks, it's 5 days by horse and wagon to the nearest train station.

Their effort to determine when the joy of their lives would walk through the front door was a total failure. They settled for the sight of a taxi pulling up in front of the house. The vigil began in earnest. Two anxious weeks later, taxi tires scraped against the curb in front of the house.

"They're here!" screamed Edith. Two pairs of bodies collided on the sidewalk, hugging and kissing all the way up the front steps and into the parlor.

That Friday, a large automobile glided to a stop in front of 349 Elm Street. Bob and Joan jumped out—Mom and Dad rushing to keep up as they bounded up the narrow path towards the front door.

George had seen the jubilant foursome from his shop and was out the back door in seconds. "You're looking for Kegham?" A chorus of yeses greeted him. "Please come in. I'm George. My sister Rose went to the church for something or other. She should be back very soon. Kegham is due home from work in an hour. I'm going to close my shop. It'll only take me a minute."

The guests made themselves at home and waited while the excitement meter pushed to its limit. The appetizing odor of food floated in from the kitchen. "You're soon to find out what baked bliss is all about, folks."

Rose noticed an automobile parked in front. The store's front door shade was down well before closing time. She entered the small living room packed with strangers.

"Rose, these are Kegham's friends all the way from Troy," quickly adding "and Khunoos."

George and Rose knew all about their mission work and their compassion and love for the Armenian people. Kegham had made sure of that many times.

Kegham spotted the familiar Stanton automobile. His stride immediately turned into a dash skipping the steps to the porch with one leap and flying through the front door into the arms of his dear friends.

The little house on Elm Street started rocking on its ancient foundation. Happy voices flowed out into the street. Passersby paused, listened, and shook their heads. "What's going on at Rose's?"

"Rose, if only you had half the size of the Stanton's dining room—especially that long table."

"George, go down to the basement and bring up the table extensions. They're under the stairs."

The round oak table expanded and seven pairs of knees and elbows happily rubbed against each other. Now, if you were under the impression that you'd leave an Armenian home without staying for a full six-course dinner, you are mistaken. It became absolutely clear that the invitation was binding and inviolate the moment you entered the house.

George proudly proclaimed, "Wait until you taste my sister's *kata*."

"Whew! We could have stopped eating an hour ago."

"Sorry, folks, that's not the Armenian way."

"Yes, Rose, I'll have another slice of kata—I've never tasted anything so delicious."

"I'll give you my recipe, Edith. Just promise not to let it go beyond your kitchen."

"I promise, Rose."

In all the excitement, it had slipped by the visitors that Troy was not a suburb of Watertown. Who cared—Bob and Bill took turns at the wheel while the ladies blissfully relaxed in the back.

For the next few weeks, there was a flood of letters between Troy and Watertown. Edith mailed some of her *kata*. Rose was amazed how well they turned out. "There had to be an Armenian somewhere in the family tree."

Kegham's world was heading towards a real-life fantasy. Everything about America worked its therapeutic effect on his tortured past. Memories of the horrors of Khunoos were fading. On occasion they would slip out of the shadows and fill the ceiling of his bedroom; on those nights it took a little longer to fall asleep.

23

Private Kegham

In the weeks before Kegham's 19th birthday,
a series of international incidents were slowly drawing
America closer into Europe's war. Even though
President Wilson had promised in his speeches that no
American soldier would go to war, on April 6, 1917,
America declared war on the Central Powers, bringing
the full power of America's industrial and military
might on the side of the Allies.

The popular ballad, "The Yanks are Coming,"
became the rallying call to thousands of eager young
Americans ready to fill the blood-soaked trenches of
the Western Front where success was measured in
yards and casualties in the thousands—wholesale
slaughter—thanks to the burgeoning advances of
modern technology.

America began a journey that would make her
the unchallenged world power for the rest of the 20th
century and beyond.

The war changed the direction of US industry.
Hood Rubber Company went on double shifts
producing everything from boots, tents, knapsacks, and
gaskets.

Kegham hadn't gone unnoticed. He was
promoted to a minor management position. The news

sent the joy-pride meter past maximum, electrifying life at 349 Elm Street.

Congratulatory telegrams from Bob and Joan and the Stantons flew over the wires. Father Levon announced the good news in church adding that after services, "Rose and George invite all their friends to their home to celebrate." Rose's eyes focused on the altar, crossed herself, and from the depths of her soul she whispered, "God bless you, my dear son."

Kata, homemade jam, coffee, tea and baklava covered the extended kitchen table. Two steady lines, one leaving with happy faces juggling plates and cups and another one eagerly shuffling in line—past the screen door and into the kitchen. "There's plenty to go around, folks."

The last to leave was Father Levon. His bag of *kata* was tucked under his arm, "How I love Rose's *kata*."

Volunteers were lining up at the recruitment centers in Watertown. Farewell parties became daily occurrences at the plant. Kegham bought Liberty War Bonds.

Soon, he would be surrounded with women and old men. His youth was becoming a serious embarrassment. He was just as much an American as those born in the US. It was time for an important decision. So, one Friday after work, Kegham walked into the superintendent's office and gave his two-week notice. Mr. Hardy smiled and congratulated Kegham adding, "You know all aliens are granted US citizenship the moment they enlist. Yes siree, that's the law. You're a full-fledged, genuine US citizen the day you enlist."

Kegham walked out of the office thinking how easy it was to leave Hood Rubber Company. "Now, how do I tell Rose and George?" The more he pondered the idea, the more they took on the status of loving parents.

Rose's keen mind sensed a change in Kegham that didn't bode well. Something was bothering her *anoushig* (darling). George had also noticed a change. The situation was becoming intolerable. Brother and sister had private talks. This change in Kegham's demeanor was becoming annoyingly unbearable.

In a determined inquiring voice, Rose asked, "When did you notice the change?"

"I think it was last Friday," answered George.

"Yes, you're right. Just after he came home from work."

Rose was going through her breakfast routine. George was in his chair at the table staring at a single *kata* crumb that Rose had missed.

Kegham finally broke the impasse. "You have never stopped showering your affection from the first day I entered your home. I could have ended in some boarding house like so many other immigrants but destiny directed me to your doorstep."

They listened and braced themselves for words that would unlock the secret they so desperately had been waiting for. Kegham continued, "You mean more to me than you can imagine." Two blank faces locked in a permanent stare, silently pleading, "Tell us what it is!"

"I'm going to join the Army! America is my country, too."

A relieved George replied, "Of course. America is your country." Before the full impact of his declaration hit them, Kegham hugged them both. He didn't want to loosen his arms and held them tight.

George forced a smile and moved towards the table. "Rose, let's have some breakfast. Our Kegham is going to be a 'general' soon." Talking, laughing, and eating brought back life to 349 Elm Street. It was clearly an illusion, only a short respite from the real feelings that would come later that night when everyone was in bed.

An uncontrollable loneliness gripped Rose. She pressed her face into the pillow, muffling the sounds of her sadness until sleep mercifully overcame her.

George thought of trenches and war. "Damn the war." Finally a restless sleep followed.

Kegham was preparing to face the next chapter of his life. That night, Rose and George dominated his thoughts. They were everywhere, on the ceiling and on the walls. He tossed and turned into an uneasy sleep.

For the next few weeks, everyone tried their best to anticipate the change that was soon to alter their lives. The dreaded special delivery letter arrived—orders to report to Camp Kilmer, New Jersey. A special train was scheduled to depart at 11 a.m. from Watertown on Thursday—only six days away.

Bob and Joan drove down from Troy when they received George's letter. They all spent Wednesday together at 349 Elm Street. Thursday, at 9 a.m., they headed for the train station. Kegham hurried over to a circle of eager young men gathered around a burly sergeant bellowing out names.

The departure time had been changed. They were to board immediately. Kegham rushed back and hugged and kissed the four dearest people in his life.

Rose stood, a pathetic lonely figure, holding a bag of *kata* crying her heart out, "God, protect my son—he is all I have. Without him life is not worth living!" Kegham didn't want to let her go.

The sergeant's hoarse voice roared—"Moving out!" From now on they were US Army property. Rose could hardly speak, "Kegham *hokis*, I'll send you *kata* every week." It was all she could say. Kegham took the bag of *kata* and kissed her one more time.

The troop train moved slowly away. From the open windows, arms waved to family and friends. Kegham waved and sent kisses. "Bye, Dr. Bob—Bye Joan—Bye, Hyreek (father)—Bye, Myreek (mother). I love you. Don't worry." The sound of the steel wheels scraping against the rails blocked out the farewells. The waving arms and smiling faces disappeared as the train changed tracks and disappeared from view. Next stop—Camp Kilmer, New Jersey.

24

Brothers Five

"One style of haircut—next!" Everyone started looking alike. "Bend over, spread your cheeks!"

"What!"

"Turn your head and cough."

Needles in both arms at the same time. "It saves time."

Dog tags—a military necklace that changes your identity to a number.

Uniforms—one style—single breasted—collar straight up the neck—one color, khaki.

Beneficiaries—mother, Rose Manoogian; father, George Manoogian. Kegham proudly printed their names and 349 Elm Street, Watertown, Massachusetts.

The next eight weeks marched by non-stop from bugle call to bugle call. Bayonet drill—"Stick that stuffed dummy like you mean it, soldier." Crawling in the mud over and under barbed wire obstacles designed to simultaneously tear uniform and flesh. Target practice—a cardboard character of a sneering enemy 50 yards away. "How could I miss?" Grenade throwing—just like pitching a baseball—"Not quite, soldier."

Army life moved at one speed—double time and meals were no exception. "Keep moving that line." "You sure can build up an appetite." "Eat as much as you want, soldier, but your tray better be clean."

Inspections—Footlockers open! Socks, belts, underwear—folded and rolled according to regulations. Bed blankets tight enough to bounce a quarter—so they say. Shoes mirror-polished, one pair on and one pair under the bed.

The recruits quickly adjusted to the changes in their lives. A few fought a losing battle to resist. The Army always won. The military had long ago determined the best philosophy. It was clear and unambiguous. The right way, the wrong way, and the army way. This is the essence of military life—yes, even the enemy's.

Graduation day—no diplomas, flowing gowns, tasseled caps, or proud parents beaming with pride. Not even a graduation dance. "What's that? We can have a party but be back from town and in bed by 11 p.m."

The band started things rolling with "The Stars and Stripes Forever." The long lines of khaki began marking time—120 steps a minute (army regulation). "Forward march" echoed down the line. Platoons merged into companies. Long columns headed for the reviewing stand packed with officers.

"Eyes straight ahead. Squint to the right—you're an inch behind—move up." Then the shrill command, "Eyes right!" The last chance to straighten the lines. Unit flags dip. The Stars and Stripes, held high, proudly passes by the reviewing officers, standing like statues, simultaneously saluting.

It's a special moment for everyone: drill sergeants, officers, generals and recruits, now bona fide soldiers.

The next step was assignment to special-unit schools. Everyone wasn't going to be sod-busting infantry. Kegham affixed a round brass badge with the letter D above crossed canons to his cap. Company D, 4th Field Artillery. Four other soldiers also were attaching the same brass badge.

The instructor's voice droned on with the streams of memorized phrases. "This is a 4.5-inch howitzer. It fires a 4.5-inch-diameter shell that weighs 48.3 lbs. Effective range 3000 yards—almost two miles. Used in close support to our lines during enemy attacks.

The team of four horses makes you highly mobile. The infantry depends on your ability to move into positions quickly to repel enemy advances into our lines. Speed and accuracy are crucial. We don't want to kill our own troops."

The five men listened attentively while examining the different parts—limber, gun carriage, caisson, etc.

Four sturdy horses patiently waited a few yards away. The instructor continued, "One man, the teamster, rides the lead horse. Two men sit on the right side of the caisson and two on the left. Note the handles on the sides of the seats. A firm grip will keep you from going airborne. Once you get rolling, you'll think you're riding the roller coaster at Coney Island."

"Private Shaw will be your teamster. " Fred had grown up on the family farm in Kentucky. He had known the gee's and haw's of horse talk since he was five years old.

"Private Stuart, you'll sweep clean the barrel after each firing." Bill Stuart was eight when his family moved from Scotland. "Private Spiros, you'll load and lock." Nick Spiros was five years old when his parents left Greece. "Robert Columbo, you'll pull the trigger." Robert Columbo was born in Buffalo, New York. His parents came from Palermo, Sicily. "Private Agegian, you will have the next shell ready to load. I want this SOB barking every ten seconds." In a few days, the howitzer was practically howling. The instructor glowed with satisfaction.

The training course covered five miles of hills, bumps, ditches, and sharp turns. Fred kept control of the horses with shouts of gee-haw combined with the subtle tugs on the reins. The men quickly learned to shift their bodies to accommodate the gravitational and centrifugal forces as they rambled and bounced "over hill and dale."

During the two weeks of training, the five young men began to forge an unbreakable bond of friendship full of trust and respect. An Armenian orphan from Khunoos had, in just over a year, found parental love and now brotherly affection.

25

Going Home

Kegham leaned his head against the cool surface of the coach window. The rhythmic clicking sounds of the train's wheels held his attention. It was late November and darkness was beginning to come earlier.

The conductor closed some of the lights leaving a faint glow. Passengers began positioning themselves for a few moments of relaxation. Kegham closed his eyes. George and Rose were seated at the little round table. Between them, his empty chair. A smile crossed his face—"I can hardly wait to see Mom and Dad." He shifted slightly into a more comfortable position.

A final burst of steam—"Watertown Station." Half walking, half running, Kegham headed for the streetcar stop. The streetcar conductor waved Kegham by—soldiers ride free. Off at 4th Street—a fast walk down Johnson Street past Saint Gregory's. Two more blocks and left on Elm Street.

Bursting with joy, an exuberant young soldier walked up the narrow pathway and quietly stepped up on the porch. The light from the kitchen was sending a portion of its glow into the parlor. Kegham carefully inserted his key into the front door. He turned it slowly, but no matter how carefully he turned the key—the inevitable click shattered the silence like a thunderbolt.

Rose's sharp ears heard. "Who's there?" The door flew open. Rose screamed something. All 160 plus pounds flew into Kegham's out-stretched arms.

A jumble of words—half finished sentences between hugs and kisses was all that Rose could do. Her *anoushik* (dearest) was home. George joined in the raucous welcoming. The little house at 349 Elm Street was again rocking on its foundation.

"Set the table, Rose." George could hardly contain himself. "Our general is home."

"*Myreek, Hyreek*, I'm home for 10 days. Those special words—mother, father—came out without hesitation and so naturally. No one paid attention. Why should they? Those words had been so often wished to be heard that it didn't matter anymore.

By 1:30 a.m., Kegham was running out of words about army life. Rose carried her son's bag into his room. "That's okay, Mom. I can unpack." George stood by the door, glowing with pride.

Rose pushed George out and closed the bedroom door. They sat at the table staring at each other, filled with an overwhelming feeling of joy and contentment. Suddenly, Rose leaped from her chair. She had forgotten to kiss her son. How awful! Too much excitement. Rose quietly opened the bedroom door. Was he sleeping? Not quite.

Rose rushed in, no pretense needed—a gentle tuck here and another there. She pushed Kegham's hair back and kissed his forehead. *"Keshair pari, Anoushik-us"* (good night, my sweet)

"Keshair pari, Myreek, Hyreek."

Kegham looked up at his familiar ceiling, closed his eyes and began reviewing all the wonderful events that led to this very moment. He tried, but it was of no use. He'd done it so many times before. His eyes started closing. "No more bugle calls, no more double time, no sergeants shouting orders. Before the brain succumbed to the sandman's wiles, there was Sergeant Rose serving slices of *kata* to a long line of eager soldiers—"That's my mom, fellas."

Kegham looked different—so grown up. George and Rose had difficulty acknowledging the change. Could it happen in just eight weeks? The ten days fell victim to the law of relativity. Kegham kissed and hugged his parents and Dr. Bob and Joan, who had come to see him off. They looked so sad and vulnerable and he felt so strong and confident.

He waved from the train's open window. The second parting was noticeably different. The first was hectic and emotional. This time it was less demonstrative but decidedly more painful.

81

26

"We're Coming Over"

The American Expeditionary Force (AEF) was rapidly growing. Its Commander in Chief, General "Black Jack" Pershing, was not about to turn his troops over to the control of French or English commanders. "Take it or leave it!" The AEF was to remain under full command of American officers.

On Christmas Eve, 1917, Company D climbed up the gang plank of the troop ship, *USS Jamestown*. New York was enshrouded in a cold, early morning mist. Further down the wharf, the howitzers and horses were also making the passenger list.

The *Jamestown* was part of a 12-ship convoy escorted by Navy destroyers. Under the Atlantic, marauding German submarines, with their periscopes cutting a foaming path just above the surface, were on the lookout to issue everyone aboard a one-way ticket to "Davey Jones' locker."

Eight uneventful days dragged by. Sturdy tug boats carefully nudged the *Jamestown* towards the mooring docks of La Havre, France. Curious soldiers leaned over the ship's railings watching busy longshoremen and the great cranes whose hooks reached into the ship's hold for the precious military cargo.

Excitement peaked when the command to "Stand by to disembark" echoed throughout the ship. The gangplank sagged and bobbed under the feet of the troops, as they shuffled single file onto French soil. The Front was getting ever closer.

Fred had named their team: Butch, Nell, Lefty, and Tag. His voice rang out to the longshoremen, "Careful with those horses!" The lieutenant waved to the teamsters to break ranks. They rushed over to their horses like protective mothers.

Without horses, the howitzers were just a useless piece of military equipment. "All present and accounted for, Sir!" Colonel Halverson acknowledged the captain's salute. "Now, where do we go from here?"

In no time, the teams, limbers, caissons, and gun carriages were hooked up. Fred kept the horses calm and relaxed. His voice and gentle tugs on the reins transmitted a feeling of confidence. Shouts of "*Vive les Américain!*" welcomed the soldiers of Company D as their caissons rumbled over the ancient cobble stone streets of La Havre towards the staging area somewhere past the city limits.

Fred shouted, "How're you guys doin' back there?"

"Buildin' calluses on top of calluses on our butts," replied Bill.

"I've had mine since I was five," answered Fred. They all chuckled. Kegham felt a feeling of pride and comradeship come over him. He was now one of five brothers.

"Happy New Year!"

"Hey, Kegham, any brothers or sisters?" Robert's innocent question failed to erupt painful memories.

"None," replied Kegham and waved at a young girl throwing kisses and flowers from a second-story window. "How about you, Bob?"

"I've a 16-year-old sister Gracie. It's just the two of us."

They continued waving at the happy faces lining the streets. Excitement was mounting. Flowers, cheers, and kisses from old and young showered on the Americans from all directions. They were being greeted like heroes—and why not? Since 1914 the Allies had lost three million dead and wounded. The sight of the young Americans, so naturally friendly and full of confidence, was coming at a time where the French and English troops needed a boost in numbers and morale.

The marshaling yards were lined with rows of boxcars and flatcars. "What? No Pullmans?"

The loading began. Five complete crews, 20 horses, and 25 men packed in a small boxcar, just one big happy family. The military hardware went first class on flatcars. By 9 p.m., Company D was on board and ready to begin the *"Tour de France."*

Fred anticipated the need of a very important item. He came back with a couple of shovels. His sharp eyes had spotted them being loaded back down the line. Fred grinned, "You're going to find out how the saying 'shoveling shit' started."

"Thanks, Fred."

"What about the rivers of piss?"

"That's why the horses are standing hoof deep in dry straw."

"Good ol' Fred."

"Ask me anything, fellas."

The little steam engine strained in a vain attempt to move forward. Its wheels spun in place, sending out streaks of bright sparks. A couple of shovels of sand thrown in front of the wheels and— voila!—traction. The couplings rattled in sequence down the line of cars as the engine picked up momentum. With a quick glance at the pressure gauge, the engineer released the throttle--Company D was on its way, 25 men and 20 horses, in a boxcar half the size of an American version.

The shoveling began in earnest. No matter how often—and they were often—the steaming piles of manure were shoveled out the car door, the odor still lingered, and when added to the urine soaked straw, left a nauseating stench penetrating the nostrils. It kept conversations down to a minimum.

The weary passengers came alive when the train slowed down after ten and a half hours non-stop. The men crowded around the door. A bright full moon, like a large celestial light bulb, illuminated the French countryside. They were at an isolated railway siding.

Whistles and commands sent the men out of their "latrine on wheels," vigorously breathing in the fresh air. Units formed in quick order.

Teamsters led their teams down the improvised wooden ramps and headed back towards the flatcars. The last shades of darkness were just a few hours away, soon to give way to a dawn that promised a clear, cold, sunny day.

A sign post a few yards away read Rheims, 14 km. Fifty miles east at US Army Headquarters, General Pershing pointed to a wall map and a pin marking the city of Rheims. Eighty miles east were the German advanced trenches and the headquarters of General Stressemann.

What's on the menu? When it came to field rations, each soldier began with the most palatable and ate down the menu. Kegham sat in his seat on the caisson watching Fred. It was obvious he enjoyed being around horses. The animals in return sensed that Fred could be trusted. The hours dragged on. Some were wondering if they hadn't gotten off at the wrong siding.

A spiral of dust in the distance and in minutes a dust-covered motorcycle screeched to a sliding stop in front of Colonel Halverson. The driver saluted, pushed up his dust-covered goggles, and handed him an envelope from his dust-covered leather pouch. A quick salute and off he went in a cloud of dust. "That's a hell of a lot of dust."

"You can say that again, soldier."

Colonel Halverson motioned to his officers, who immediately gathered around him. A brief exchange of words; they saluted and returned to their units. Lieutenant Schroeder's voice was loud and clear, "Moving out in 15 minutes." Relief generates its own brand of motivation.

Men, horses, and howitzers were ready in record time. One more move, about fifteen miles down the tracks near the city of Rheims. Excitement was mounting. "Oh! What I'd do for a hot meal."

27

Getting Closer

The field kitchens were in place , ready to serve the army's gourmet special. "But first, gentlemen, let us sing in praise of what we are about to eat. You all know the words—just follow the bouncing white ball on the screen:"

"Beans, beans, the musical fruit.

The more you eat, the more you toot.

The more you toot, the better you feel,

So let's have beans for every meal. Amen.

Pass the hard tack, pal."

Kegham had a moment of fantasy. The kitchen table at 349 Elm Street with three people seated, laughing, talking, and eating. Fred's voice dominated the moment, "Hey fellows, if we run out of shells, we can use these biscuits. They're hard as rock!"

Someone shouted, "Petrified dough!"

Busy hands dipped the biscuits into mess kits filled with beans floating in tomato sauce. The coffee was hot and black.

Pup tents started to pop up like mushrooms after a rain. The troops prepared to settle down for the night. Teamsters were busy curry-brushing their teams. Some letter writing, a poker game with cigarettes for chips, small groups talking, a few in their tents trying out their military mattress— blanket over terra firma.

The celestial light bulb was back, casting its beams on a sea of tents. Sentries were posted. The headquarters tent was aglow. Inside, shadows moved about planning for tomorrow.

Two sentries turned their eyes in the direction of the front. The flashes of light streaking in the distance illuminated the darkened horizon followed by the sounds of booming cannons sent an unmistakable message—but it was lost in a moment of wishful thinking. "Looks like rain, Joe."

"Yeah, I'm not much for snow."

28

Corporal Fred

Company D was a part of the American units assigned to a 15-mile section of the front near Chateau Thierry where weary Royal Highland Fusiliers and other British units had been exchanging trenches with the enemy for the past two and a half years.

Trench warfare breeds an insidious, demoralizing hopelessness of days and nights spent in narrow trenches with vermin, fleas, filth, and just a few yards away the stench of the decaying corpses of friend and foe lying in no-man's land. It was an experience that would haunt the survivors for years.

During periods of snow and rain, the men huddled in primitive, underground, makeshift shelters, dirty, unshaven, and emotionally drained, watching for the next enemy onslaught that never failed to come. A senseless and deadly exercise in futility.

A never-ending cycle: repel, advance, and retreat. "Weren't we in this trench last week?" "No, the trench we were in last week is over there—the Germans are there now. We're in the one they were in last week."

Thus was trench warfare on the Western Front—senseless, stupid, and insane—and it had to stop. The Yanks had come to put an end to the madness.

Fresh, untested Americans filled the battle-scarred trenches eager to bring the Hun to his knees. The unfolding of events was rapidly building for a last and decisive effort to bring to an end the slaughter of a whole generation of young men on both sides of the conflict.

The American sector was ready and in place. The war-weary Germans would soon find out on whose side the forces of destiny would favor.

The troops of Company D spent the next three days checking and rechecking their equipment. Colonel Halverson expected nothing less than perfection. The men responded with respect to their colonel, a graduate of West Point, and the only son of a Swedish immigrant family from a small Minnesota farming community.

The men knew him as fair, firm, and fearless. The latter character trait would soon show itself in the heat of battle.

Bill inquired if anyone had seen Fred since breakfast. Nick thought he saw him heading over to the horses with their feed bags. He went to check. Butch, Nell, Lefty, and Tag were enjoying their feed bags, but Fred was nowhere in sight.

However, at the other end of the encampment, an unusual scene was developing. Several French women, seated behind sewing machines, were busy pedaling their "Singers" as they sewed corporal stripes

91

on shirts, jackets, and fatigues. If BVDs had sleeves, they would have sewn stripes on them.

The teamsters were being promoted en mass. Colonel Halverson was establishing the last link in the chain of command. Corporal Fred Shaw faced the gaze of his buddies. In the next few hours, the men had a field day responding to the sudden promotions, saluting at every opportunity. "Yes, Sir!" "No, Sir!" "Sir, may I be excused to take a piss—sorry, Sir—I mean urinate."

A stern unequivocal "No!" followed.

"But Sir, my bladder is about to burst!"

"Okay, but don't let it happen again." Waves of laughter. It wasn't long before everything was back to normal.

29

The General Speaks

Colonel Halverson returned from General Headquarters with the battle orders for Company D. Three days earlier all commanders had assembled in a converted school room to listen to General Pershing's explanation of how the American forces were to defend their sector of the front. A large operational wall map prominently displayed a section of shaded areas. General Pershing's pointer moved between quadrants L4 and L8. "This area is approximately 100 miles of the front." He paused long enough for the officers to check the shaded areas of their unit's positions.

General "Black Jack" Pershing was a no-nonsense, straightforward officer all his military life, clear in his pronouncements, unwavering in his beliefs, having an inborn character trait that never lost sight of the forces of reality. He continued, "Our allies have been fighting a war of attrition for over 3 years. Their troops are weary and low in morale, but so are the Germans. The German soldier is dedicated, brave, and tenacious. He has proven time and again that he can go that extra mile when ordered.

Our troops are well equipped and trained. Their morale is high and full of enthusiasm that's uniquely American. You all know what I mean. We all grew up with that same brand of enthusiasm. I don't want our men to learn the hard way. Every effort has to be exerted to prevent over-confidence and foolhardy acts. The future of our troops is in your hands. Command wisely. Always uphold the honor of the US Army no matter what the circumstances."

General Pershing paused and looked at his field commanders with deliberate eye contact. A moment of quiet descended over the group in the dimly lit school room. Only the faint distant rumblings from the front broke the silence. There was no more to be said. The officers saluted and filed out. The general's heart ached knowing full well the consequences that lay ahead and the price that would have to be paid for victory. He sat down and focused his eyes on the shaded areas on the map, lost in thought.

30

In Position

Company D's orders were to position their guns so that concentrated crossfire could be maintained as close as possible near the sector of the American trenches. Army intelligence reported the arrival of fresh German units. Something was brewing and it wasn't beer.

Tense, wide-eyed, green American infantrymen lined the meandering trenches straining their eyes across the desolate battle-scarred landscape towards the German lines five miles away.

The stress-filled air had its moments of hilarity. "Men make sure your bladders are empty. There'll be no time to take a piss once the show starts. I don't want to see or smell squads of piss-soaked britches. Is that clear?" From a lone, hesitant, timid voice from somewhere down the line... "Yes, sarg."

"Under no condition will you crap in your pants. You all know the foul smell army rations produce. We don't want to gas our own men—do we? Let me hear it!"

A chorus of voices rolled down the trenches, "Yes, sir, sarg."

"If you're going to die, do it with dry pants front and back." Anything to lower the tension meter down to "bearable."

By 3 a.m., Company D's howitzers were in their staggered positions. Fred hobbled the team a few yards away —hopefully out of harm's way. Fred was a professional scrounger. How he got so many apples no one would ever know. Crackling, crunching, the apples quickly disappeared. Fred gently patted Butch, Nell, Lefty, and Tag who gratefully whinnied their thanks.

"Hey, Fred, where's our apples?" shouted Bill.

"When you can pull 4000 pounds of equipment over hill and dale, then you'll get apples," answered Fred.

"Are all Kentucks quick on answers?" Bill tweaked in response.

"Yep," answered Fred, "I reckon I'm slower than most."

31

Act One

Seven a.m.—the shrill sounds of enemy shells passed overhead. One landed in an open area and left a large, gaping hole. In seconds, the sounds of whistling shells were going in both directions.

The duel lasted about 15 minutes. A few final bursts and then silence. Several direct hits on the trenches started a premature body count. The wounded were rushed to field hospitals and the dead buried in hastily prepared graves.

"No sight of the enemy, and we're already collecting dog tags." An eerie silence spread down the trenches. "Welcome to the front, boys."

"Look! There's a bird on that tree. Doesn't it know there's a war going on?"

"God, I wish I was a bird."

Eyes strained between sand bags looking for the assault that was supposed to follow the bombardment. "Don't they know we're waiting with machine guns? Idiots, you're easy targets at 600 feet."

"Listen, buddy, they've been doing this for the last 3 years."

"Good grief, I need to take a pee."

"Don't forget to flush."

Charged, nervous laughter relieved tightened muscles, if only for a few moments. Then it was back to peering between sand bags for those advancing gray uniforms with fixed bayonets.

Kegham gave Bob a half-hearted smile, who responded with a thumbs-up. Fred kept a close watch on his horses. Nick finished counting the shells wrapped in their wicker tubes. "100—that's about 25 minutes of steady barking," mused Nick. Dark clouds were moving in from the east, chilling the air.

Colonel Halverson studied the names of the casualties, folded the sheet and slipped it into his pocket. He then sent a runner with orders to tighten the line of howitzers. Word came down the line that Company D had lost 7 dead and 12 wounded. "Good grief! We've yet to see the enemy."

32

The Plan

The orderly rushed past groups of staff officers, clicked his heels, and snapped to attention. He handed the general another intelligence report. The general pressed his monocle against his eye and began reading. "No signs of American troop movements out of Rheims. Next report at 7:30 a.m."

General Otto Stressemann was honed and shaped in the Prussian military tradition, a system of military training begun two centuries ago by Frederick the Great of Prussia. He stood straight and rigid as a steel beam. He was thorough and unyielding once a decision was made. His expressionless, cold demeanor excluded opinions from subordinates—listen and obey were their only options.

General Stressemann saw war as the epitome of the game of chess. Every move, calculated to control the board to keep your opponent on the defensive until the one miscalculated move that would end in checkmate.

He affixed his monocle and moved towards the large map spread across the table, studying it carefully and methodically. There were still a few more moves to be made. His staff officers stood and watched their general. The moment to listen and obey was slowly approaching.

Plan "Hammer" was to draw the Americans out of Rheims towards Neveau—a small city on the road to Paris. He hoped to accomplish this by sending General von Kreutzer's Fourth Army in a slow, deliberate march towards Neveau, for an all-out drive on Paris—at least that was how it was to appear. The Krupp Company's long range guns, dubbed "Big Bertha" after Herr Krupp's wife, were already dropping their calling card on Paris every fifteen minutes from seventy miles away.

When the Americans were at least fifty miles out of Rheims, General Schleicher's Army West would strike the American's weakened lines. The American troops on the road to Neveau would be too far away to return in time to join their counterparts.

General von Kreutzer's Fourth Army would turn back from their supposed attack on Paris and in forced march reach General Schleicher's Army West for a joint attack on Rheims and on to La Havre, the vital port supplying the AEF. The port would be in German hands and no matter how brave or well led, no army can sustain itself in battle without supplies—checkmate.

33

Listen, Learn, and Live

10 p.m. – The full moon was only a faint glow behind a translucent, low, overcast sky. Ideal conditions for the snipers' deadly business. German snipers cautiously inched their way from shell hole to shell hole until reaching a favorable location and patiently waited to focus on their target through powerful Zeiss telescopic lenses.

Sergeant Donovan decided to hold night classes for the green troops of his platoon. "Gentlemen, a sniper only needs a few inches of your head to be visible and death comes swiftly and painlessly." As he spoke, he scanned the faces of the recruits. Some looked uninterested; a few were not sure what to do. Donovan continued, "All snipers, no matter which army, are feared and hated. They don't fight in the open like the rest of us dumb bastards. So be careful." Some signs of interest were beginning to surface. Encouraged, Donovan continued, "You might want to take a peek one day, just out of curiosity— don't." A few turned to light cigarettes. The sergeant was losing the attention of his class. Some hands-on training was in order. "All right, children, it's 'show-and-tell time.' Let's see if we have any company out there." Taking the helmet from one of the soldiers, he perched it at the end of a bayonet. This generated curiosity from the students who started to show interest as in a class when an experiment is being

101

performed by the teacher. A few moved in closer. The skeptics held their places as if to say, "There's a sucker born every minute and here's a trench full of them."

The sergeant slowly lifted the helmet towards the top of the sandbags lining the trench. Eyes followed the helmet as it was slowly exposed just inches above the sandbags. Down and up, side to side, ever so slowly—nothing happened. Now one hundred percent of the students were convinced that their legs were being pulled right out of their sockets—the teacher began a second attempt. This time, he held the helmet slightly higher—a little more accommodating. Zip! Ping!

Eyes popped; cigarettes dropped free fall from open mouths—one hundred percent believers rushed crouching around the sergeant. A satisfied Donovan turned to the helmet's owner, "Show your buddies how close you came to cashing in your chips, soldier."

The lesson continued—the classroom was filling with true believers. "It would have gone right through your temple, Jack." Another Zip! And sand poured out of a bag just above the peep hole.

A broad grin covered the sergeant's face. "This guy's really good and he wants you to know it. He's a real pro—ya gotta give him credit." End of class. "I need to take a piss. Anyone want to join me?"

"If the Sarg says piss, I'm pissing." The teacher had the full confidence of his students from that moment on.

At another section of the trenches, the sniper's rifle sent its deadly greeting to a careless soldier whose curiosity had got the best of him. Another responded with foolish bravado by standing on an empty ammunition box threatening to fire his rifle. The three-second hero's last words were, "You sneaky kraut son-of-a-bitch!" Zip! Ping! Right above the right eye. Two soldiers learned the hard way. Their buddies stood motionless, gasping as blood and brain poured out of the head of the hapless soldier. "Fella's, just wait until the shooting really starts." The cold January night was having its effect on the troops, but they weren't shivering because of the chilled air.

34

Your Move, Herr General

US Army Headquarters at Rheims was busy analyzing the steady stream of reports about General von Kreutzer's Fourth Army movements. All information pointed towards a drive towards Neveau and then on to Paris.

It was a gamble but if successful, it would put the Germans in a strong enough position to bring the war to a quick and decisive end and before the full might of the AEF could be brought to bear on the weary and exhausted Kaiser's Army.

General Pershing picked up the phone. General Hathaway was reporting: "I'm sure Neveau is their objective." General Pershing paused, "Thanks, Hathaway—check back in 30 minutes."

His tactician's mind was racing. Hesitation could have catastrophic consequences but a hurried response had its own inherent dangers. Pershing huddled with his staff. A few minutes of discussion in a sober and relaxed manner followed.

The field phone rang precisely on time. "Hathaway, move as many companies as you can to Neveau. The French are waiting. We'll help all we can from this end."

"Thanks, Jack," came the reply.

"Give them hell, Stan."

"Yes, Sir!"

Both men were classmates at West Point 30 years earlier.

Reports were coming in with greater frequency. General Stressemann read them with growing satisfaction. American troops were beginning to pull out of the Rheims sector towards Neveau on the road to Paris.

In a few days, they will have advanced well out of Rheims, at which point they would be unable to return in time to defend the outnumbered American forces. Von Kreutzer's Fourth and Schleicher's Army West will have joined forces, taken Rheims and on to the port at Le Havre, the AEF's main source of supplies. Germany had to bring the war to a rapid and decisive end before the strength of the AEF tipped the balance in favor of the Allies.

35

Rumors

Rumors of large troop movements spread up and down the American sector. Colonel Halverson left for GHQ earlier that morning. There is nothing more exhilaratingly contagious than rumors confirming rumors. One thing was certain, something important was about to take place that would end the grinding stagnation infecting the troops. The field artillery units nervously waited for the orders that would free them from the flood of rumors spilling over from the trenches.

Fred covered the team with several large canvas tarpaulins. Again, Fred would produce things out of thin air. He never ceased to get his brothers' admiration. Each team member's talents bonded the brothers ever closer.

Kegham was in his pup tent preparing to write a letter home. Dear Mother and Father—he paused and stared out at the steady precipitation of large wet snowflakes that melted as soon as they landed. Moments of melancholy were always to be a part of his emotional make-up. Unexpected sadness would creep over him without warning. Kegham indulged in a moment of fantasy. There was the cozy kitchen at 349 Elm Street—all four burners with steaming pots of Rose's best. His imagination started to play tricks. He thought he smelled freshly baked *kata*.

36

Final Move

Several days dragged by without a hint of a German attack. February was turning the American sector into a sea of mud and pools of dank smelling water fed by the wet snowflakes.

The damp, penetrating chill played havoc in the trenches. Troops took turns sitting or standing, shuffling their feet in mud while others focused their weary eyes between sandbags. The heavy mist, low clouds, and falling snow brought visibility down to a few hundred feet. German intelligence reported that General Hathaway's troops were approaching the half way mark on the road to Neveau. General Stressemann motioned his staff over. He was ready to make his last move before "checkmate."

The staff officers couldn't resist showing visible signs of elation. The general's monocle was framed by tight face muscles. A Prussian officer never displays emotion—a military machine has none.

His trim figure, neatly filling a finely-tailored uniform, stood like a pillar of strength radiating stability, competence, and confidence. Orders were sent to General von Kreutzer to join Schleicher for the attack on the weakened American sectors. From now on the American reaction had to be constantly monitored. German intelligence would be on high alert for the next critical hours.

37

Change in Plans

A Spad fighter plane from America's "Hat in the Ring" Squadron roared over, banked low into a steep turn and dropped a message canister. In seconds, General Hathaway was reading its contents. "Immediately—turn back to Rheims—von Kreutzer and Schleicher joining to attack Rheims. Neveau was a ploy." Pershing.

An immediate halt was ordered. The troops took to the sides of the road. The rumor mill began in full force spreading up and down the lines.

General Hathaway wrote a hasty note and sent a runner to fetch Master Sergeant Crawford. The officers gathered on a small rise of land facing their General. Their faces mirrored an intense anticipation that a drastic change in plans was forthcoming.

The General was deeply absorbed with the logistics of the change in plans. He read the contents of the order—a few officers started moving, anticipating what was to follow.

General Hathaway waved them back. "Hold it, gentlemen; we're not going back to Rheims." The officers closed ranks in a tight ring around their commander. Out of nowhere, Master Sergeant Crawford, bobbing and wobbling on a very large draft horse, came on the scene. He slid off the horse and snapped to attention. "Reporting as ordered, Sir!" The scene of horse and rider captured the attention of everyone.

General Hathaway, an ex-cavalry officer, stared at the huge horse. The sergeant anticipated the General's thoughts. "I got him from a very nice farmer…over there," pointing his hand out into space. What he meant was that he took the animal when no one was looking.

The horse had a simple rope, bit, and brace, and no saddle. Draft horses are never saddled. General Hathaway squeezed out a smile. "Sergeant, have you ever ridden—he almost said house—a horse bareback?"

"No, sir, on both counts."

General Hathaway continued in a friendly familiar tone. "Be careful Joe, don't fall and break your neck. You've got a lot of distance to cover." He gave him the canister with his reply to Pershing. "You've got to get to Rheims in less than thirty hours."

"Yes, Sir, don't you fret, Sir," and with determined effort he mounted and dug his heels into the horse's enormous ribs, pounding with great force until the animal got the message and began a slow trot.

The troops looked in wonderment at the comic scene. "What in the hell is that man doing on that horse?" Rumors spread with the fury of wildfires— but not for long.

General Hathaway presented his change in plan, a forced march straight towards von Kreutzer's Fourth Army. Cut him off from joining Schleicher's Army West. Uncomplicated but required total commitment from all ranks. Hathaway continued, "I realize our troops are tired from almost four days of forced marching with very little rest. I'm asking for all of us to give an all-out effort to intercept the enemy before they join forces."

A voice from the group interrupted, "We can do it, Sir! I hope the sergeant doesn't fall off that beast and break his neck." Plenty of laughter – the tonic that makes being human a unique pleasure.

"Thank you, gentlemen."

38

Now or Never

In less than twenty-eight hours, an exhausted, weary Sergeant Crawford and a panting, breathless horse reached headquarters. Every one of the sergeant's 208 bones was crying out, "Never again!"

As General Pershing read Hathaway's plan, it was clear to the Commander-in-Chief what the General was proposing. Revised battle plans started swirling around in his head as he moved towards the wall map of the front.

At that very moment, Hathaway's troops were approaching von Kreutzer's rear units. It wouldn't be long before von Kreutzer would have to stop and take defensive action. This meant delaying his rendezvous with General Schleicher.

General Hathaway's decision to "change" General Pershing's orders threw Stressemann's game plans into extra moves. Von Kreutzer was forced to slow down linking up with Schleicher. The unexpected turn of events put the Germans in a quandary. Time was now a critical factor for both sides. The clock was ticking. The center of the chess board was up for grabs.

General Schleicher had no choice but to begin his heavy artillery barrage. Explosions rocked the front. The dreaded order, "fix bayonets!" echoed down the German trenches. Untested doughboys girded themselves for the impending battle.

Colonel Halverson sent runners to all his cannoneers, "Hold present positions." The American front was narrowed down to three miles.

Eyes strained, scanning no-man's land for signs of the enemy. The barrage exchange continued with no letup. The screeching sounds of shells overhead added to the tension. The agonized screams of the wounded added its sobering effects on the living.

Less than a half day's march away, General Hathaway's troops were decimating von Kreutzer's rear guard units. Fritz was eagerly shouting, "*Kamaraden!*" The growing number of prisoners was causing a logistical problem. It was preventing Hathaway from fully engaging von Kreutzer's advanced troops.

General von Kreutzer was forced to salvage the main body of his troops in order to join General Schleicher, leaving his rear guard units to their fate. There was still a chance for a German victory.

5:30 a.m., the shelling stopped. Kreutzer's reduced force reached Schleicher's Army West and in an abandoned farm house the two generals finalized their revised attack plans. An all-out drive was the only solution. It had to be quick and decisive.

39

Retreat!

The tempo of anxiety on the impending battle spread up and down the American lines. Each soldier displayed only the surface of his deepest feelings. Each man's true nature would surface according to the circumstances and demands of the unfolding events that were soon to envelop them.

Some would discover character traits they never knew they possessed and silently take a measure of pride. Others would, in shameful silence, try to forget their cowardly acts, but never be able to fully obliterate them from memory. The fundamental human trait that guides all actions is the primitive urge to stay alive.

6:00 a.m.: German snipers began their ritual of death by stealth, seeking out the careless few.

7:00 a.m.: The full force of Schleicher's Army West, plus over half of Kreutzer's 4th Army, opened the massive drive towards the American lines.

Well-coordinated units of experienced and battle-hardened German troops had to first cover several miles of no-man's land before reaching within rifle range of the American trenches. German artillery began its continuous barrage tearing gaps in the American lines. Field hospitals were busy with the injured. It was estimated that in less than two hours, the advancing enemy infantry would be in sight.

Fred kept his eye on his team hobbled a few yards away, so tense and excited. Company D's howitzers barked down the line. An explosion shook the earth. "Where in the hell did that come from?" shouted Bill. Hot shrapnel pierced the air. No one would ever know how close to death they were in that fleeting moment.

Fred ran towards his team. Nell and Lefty were down quivering and shaking. From open gashes of torn flesh and shattered bones flowed torrents of blood. Fred instantly reacted with two quick shots, mercifully ending their suffering.

Fred removed the hobbles from the trembling Butch and Tag and led them to a safer area. The enemy barrage was accurate and deadly. Stretcher bearers rushed, picking up mangled bodies spilling their life's blood—many were never to reach the field hospital alive.

Kegham's body was visibly trembling. He was standing in his father's blood: Mariam's pitiful cries—Baby Victoria's screams—Setrak's pleading voice, "Myreek! Myreek!" Bob shouted, "Kegham! Are you okay?"

Another close explosion. Shrapnel filled the air. Nick grabbed his shoulder shouting something in

Greek. Lines of pain streaked across his face. Fred shouted, "Medic!"

"I'm not leaving, Fred!" His comrades rushed to their brother's side. There was nothing they could say to this stubborn Greek kid.

The battle raged all along the front. Machine guns spit out torrents of death. Several efforts to break the American defenses met with stubborn costly resistance. Hand-to-hand fighting blunted every attempt. A short lull followed. Time for both sides to plan, regroup, and start again. The clock kept ticking, bringing the climactic end ever closer.

Fred motioned to Bill to follow him. "We'll be right back, fellas," were Fred's parting words as they headed toward the rest of Company D's cannoneers. They passed shattered twisted metal and splintered wood. Soldiers lay scattered in gruesome positions, some dead, some groaning with pain, while others silently endured their injuries. Stretcher bearers rushed, collecting dog tags from corpses.

Fred's thoughts were working overtime. "I think we've got enough cannoneers to keep a strong stable line." "Right, Fred," responded Bill. Fred continued, "There's enough horses left to make the move." Bill was sure that Fred was ready to spring one of his "out-of-the-hat tricks."

At field headquarters, Colonel Halverson reluctantly read the orders to move Company D back to new defense positions. "Retreat." The word stoked hot coals of anger inside him.

The enemy was getting the advantage. The next push could be devastating to the Americans. Forward trenches were being evacuated to new rear defensive positions.

The breathless headquarters' runner paused to catch his breath. "Orders—pull back immediately." Bob, Nick, and Kegham were sitting, leaning against the caisson, staring at the dead horses a few yards away. They didn't look up or acknowledge the runner. They weren't about to leave without Fred and Bill.

The remaining cannoneers were gathered around Fred when the runner approached—he repeated the orders. Fred shouted, "Pull back—you mean retreat?! Bullshit! We're staying!" His voice was clear and emphatic.

Bill chimed in, "You heard the man. We're not budging." From the looks on the faces of the other men, it was unanimous. The puzzled runner started back, with overtaxed lungs, to headquarters. How was he going to report?

Fred faced his fellow cannoneers. They were ready to listen. Their dues had been paid for the right to disobey. The rows of dead comrades were reason enough. Gathering his thoughts, Fred faced the men who had just placed their lives into his hands. In times of crises, latent talents rise to the fore without prompting. So it was with Corporal Fred Shaw. His ability to quickly evaluate and take appropriate action was fortified by an unwavering self-confidence.

For the next hour, the remaining crews repositioned their guns. His brothers knew of Fred's resourcefulness, but to their amazement and pride, they found out that this Kentucky farm boy was a natural leader. He was calm and unassuming in manner, and clear in objective. The men followed willingly without questioning his orders.

"General Pershing—Sir. If you need another general, we would like to recommend Corporal Fred Shaw, Company D."

40

"Bullshit!"

Events were rapidly unfolding. The combined forces of the two German armies outnumbered the Americans. A few hours away, General Hathaway's exhausted troops pushed their weary bodies in an all-out effort to catch up with von Kreutzer's 4th Army, not knowing that they had already joined Schleicher's Army West.

General Hathaway was also unaware that the Americans had pulled back to secondary positions. Time was fast becoming a precious commodity for both sides.

General Hathaway's calculations for success came down to General Pershing's forces to stall the Germans long enough for their combined forces to form a pincer movement and blunt the German drive. This hope drove General Hathaway towards the climactic battle just hours away.

The events cascaded unabated. The combatants fearfully waited for the eventual carnage that would test the reactions of every man from private to general.

The runner, gasping for air—his chest heaving with each breath, reported, "Sir, b…b…b…bullshit!" quickly adding, "That's what the Company D corporal said, Sir!"

General Pershing stared wide-eyed and to everyone's amazement, a tight grin appeared only to quickly disappear. The general turned toward the wall map and concentrated on the colored pins indicating Company D's positions.

"Bullshit!" This time the smile was hidden behind the general's military bearing. He silently remembered his own words—"Every effort must be exerted to prevent over confidence and foolhardy acts."

41

Surprise Visitor

Fred's band of "mutineers" finished moving into their new positions. Crews were reduced to four per gun so as to get full use of the remaining howitzers. German runners brought word that Hathaway's troops were being strafed by German aircraft less than three miles away.

The forces of desperation were closing ranks with devastating effect on von Kreutzer and Schleicher.

Nick tried to lift a shell but the pain in his shoulder was overwhelming. Kegham improvised a sling out of a blanket which helped to ease the pain.

Fred sized up Nick. "Do you think you can get up that tree and be our eyes and help direct fire?" The answer was instantaneous—"Just get me up there, Fred."

Kegham climbed as high as possible, hung a rope over a sturdy branch, and dropped it down. Fred made a loop big enough to hold Nick's feet. Then, on signal, Kegham grasped the rope and, while the three brothers pulled Nick up, he became the counter weight.

Nick partially hid behind a branch full of dry leaves—perfect cover. "I can see over a mile," an enthusiastic Nick shouted from his perch.

"Terrific, Nick!" replied Fred.

After several miles of jarring and bouncing in a motorcycle sidecar and then continuing on foot over slippery, snow-covered shell holes, a breathless, perspiring Colonel Halverson staggered into view. The look imprinted on his face left no doubt as to what was to follow. The sting of reprimand was about to be felt by the men of Company D.

Bob, Bill, Kegham, and Fred snapped to attention, their eyes riveted straight ahead. Seconds more of heavy breathing and after wiping oceans of perspiration, the colonel shouted, "Who's the S.O.B. who told the headquarters' runner 'Bullshit?!'"

His voice boomed down the line of cannoneers. The men silently waited for their commander's growing anger to envelop them. The shrill sound of an approaching enemy shell would have been most welcome. Instead, a voice from on high came the answer. "Corporal Fred Shaw is the S.O.B., Colonel Halverson—Sir, and we're the rest of the S.O.B.s."

A totally bewildered Colonel Halverson stared up at Nick straddling a branch, with his arm in a blood soaked sling, smiling down at his perplexed commander.

Colonel Halverson, still catching his breath, took another look down the line of cannoneers who were all waving and beaming smiles. A quick glance up at Nick; the colonel turned to Fred and in a loud clear voice—"Corporal, could you use another S.O.B.?"

The shouts from the men that followed felt like they were back cheering their home team. Was that possible?

Moments like this can never be replicated. Their reaction to the unfolding of events would be remembered for a long time.

Nick's excited voice broke the cheering below. "I can see movement about a mile away." Fred turned towards his colonel who, without hesitation, flashed a reassuring smile.

42

Checkmate, Herr General

The moment of convergence of the two armies
was racing towards its terrifying climax. Soon
families back home would be left with only faint
memories of their loved one's parting words, warm
embraces, and their last farewells from the open train
windows.

Sadness and melancholy were overcoming
Kegham; he wanted so much to see Rose and George
just one more time, to walk down the narrow pathway,
through the front door of 349 Elm Street and shout,
"Mom! Dad! I'm home!"

Nick's excited voice brought Kegham back to
reality. "Fred—they're coming into range—2500
yards in three waves about a fourth of a mile apart!"

Fred shouted, "Your orders, Sir!"

"Whenever you're ready, Corporal Shaw,"
Fred snapped to attention, "Yes, Sir! We're going to
fire for range accuracy, Nick." "Fire away, Freddie!"

A single howitzer barked. Its shell exploded in
front of the advancing German troops. Nick's excited
voice continued, "Trajectory up five degrees and
sweep to the right about eight degrees, Fred!" The line
of howitzers corrected their aim and began sending
their welcome to a surprised enemy. According to
German intelligence, the Americans had drawn back to

secondary positions. How did they miss these "*schwinehunds*?"

All along the advancing lines of German infantry, orders were issued to halt and dig in. The Germans were still short of rifle range.

Colonel Halverson motioned to Fred who immediately rushed to his side. "Corporal, I think they'll be training their guns on our positions very soon now." In minutes the remaining team of horses moved the guns to their new positions. In no time, several enemy shells left gaping holes near the area they had vacated.

Kegham and Bob rushed to bring Nick down. A sniper's bullet hit Bob's thigh. He dropped, screaming in pain. Kegham hugged the ground. The tree was about 25 feet away. Kegham looked up, "Nick, don't try anything foolish." Kegham rushed over to Bob. Bullets whizzed by. They reached safety behind a caisson.

Kegham cautiously crawled towards the tree. Nick already had his feet in the loop. Kegham stood up to get a firmer grip on the rope. Nick was about ten feet from the ground when the sniper made his second hit. Kegham's chest oozed blood. He fell but kept his grip on the rope until Nick was safely down. Nick's frantic voice cried out, "Kegham, Kegham!" and fell over his brother's body to protect him. A bullet hit the tree above Nick's head. Another whizzed by to the right, and another to the left. Colonel Halverson, Bill, and Fred rushed to Nick's side. In seconds, Kegham was placed next to Bob. More bullets sent their deadly message.

In less than an hour, the German infantry, bayonets fixed, began moving across the three-mile front. Company D's howitzers were relentlessly barking, slowing the enemy's effort to reach the American trenches. American machine gunners spit death each time the Germans came into range.

General Hathaway's troops began driving in from the northwest. General Pershing slowly closed the pincers' movement from the southeast. The inferno continued into the night. Efforts to break the American line failed at great cost to the Germans. The pincers' crossfire wreaked havoc on the enemy.

By daybreak, the last-gasp effort of the attackers felt the full might of American cross-fire. The German will to continue to fight was broken. The battlefield sounds of death and destruction gave way to the sorrowful cries of the wounded. Growing numbers of bewildered Germans, their hands raised, stumbled towards the American lines while others helped their wounded comrades. The defeated enemy had suddenly become a pathetic, helpless human being seeking help. The victors reached out to help. The paradox that haunts all combatants—the futility of war was everywhere.

43

Fast Fred

Fred and Bill fashioned a blanket into
a makeshift stretcher and rushed an unconscious
bleeding Kegham to the field hospital a few miles
away. Company D had two howitzers left, and three
horses hobbled under a tree. Butch and Nell didn't
survive. The falling snow would soon cover their
bodies, along with the dead of both sides.

The scene at the field hospital overwhelmed
both brothers. Fred's voice was charged with anger.
"Bill, there must be a football field of stretchers out
there!" Bill shook his head in amazement at the sight.
The gently falling snow was slowly blanketing the
rows of wounded men. The brothers stood spellbound.
They laid Kegham, still unconscious, gently on the
ground. Their hands were cold and numb. Exhaustion
from moving non-stop for nearly an hour had taxed
their strength to continue.

Fred's searching eyes spotted an empty
stretcher. In seconds, Kegham was off the ground in
a more comfortable position. There was no doubt in
Fred's mind that Kegham was going to get immediate
attention and not end up laid out in one of the neat
rows of stretchers crying in pain, or gasping his last
breath.

Bill's anxious eyes looked towards Fred. "We
can't wait—Kegham has lost a lot of blood. He's

probably already in shock." In silent agreement they placed their army coats over their brother.

Fred intensified his efforts to get immediate help. His alert eyes noticed that stretchers with red tags went straight to one of the emergency operating tents. "I'll be right back." A smile crossed Bill's face—Fred has found the solution.

Fred rushed towards two stretcher bearers carrying a red-tagged, injured soldier timing himself just as they were entering the operating tent. "We're out of tags," he solemnly whispered as the injured soldier was lifted on the operating table minus the red tag.

Fred quickly returned to a jubilant Bill. "You're too much, Fred."

"I know, Bill," responded Fred with a wink. Next step was to locate an empty operating table. They carried Kegham down the row of tents desperately looking for one. They got to the entrance of a tent one step ahead of another wounded soldier whose bearers rushed off to find another empty operating table.

The weary army doctor, in blood stained apron, approached his next patient. After a routine appraisal, the operating team began their work salvaging another broken body.

In an hour, the last stitch was knotted and cut. The sniper's bullet had just missed Kegham's heart, passed by his spinal column, and lodged in his shoulder blade, shattering it into several small splinters.

The surgeon rubbed his eyes with the back of his hand—"Station 2" were his next words which sounded more like "Next" at the grocery counter. That sent Fred and Bill straight to Kegham's side and with the help of two medics, gently placed Kegham back on the stretcher.

Kegham was still under the effects of the anesthetic, but in a second of semi-consciousness, he looked up at his two brothers. Was it a dream? Was he dead? It didn't matter.

"Where's Station 2?" asked Fred. The medic pointed to a line of ambulances, their engines running. They placed Kegham safely on board. Fred turned to the driver, "We've been ordered to help at Recovery." Bill reveled at Fred's operating techniques.

The two brothers accompanied Kegham, one on the running board and the other holding the canopy strut of the Model T Ford ambulance as they rumbled towards the hospital. Fred gave Bill a thumbs up while silently singing, "Over hill, over dale, we'll hit the dusty trail, as those caissons go rolling along."

Bill's silent praise was, "Fred, you did it again."

44

Brothers Five, All Alive

Of the original 125 men of Company D, 30 had survived. Their decision to hold their position helped to keep the enemy from moving up. In effect, it gave the two American forces enough time to close their pincers movement and deliver their own checkmate

In a few weeks, replacements would bring Company D up to full strength. Colonel Halverson ordered field promotions: Corporal Fred was promoted to Second Lieutenant Shaw, and Private Bill to Staff Sergeant Stuart.

The day of their promotions, Fred looked at Bill and in a mock authoritarian voice said, "Sergeant Stuart, now that I'm an officer and a gentleman, if you ever 'sir' me when we're alone, I'll kick your ass so hard you'll think it was a Kentucky mule."

Bill quickly snapped to attention, saluted, and replied, "Yes Siree...Freddie dear." Unabated laughter filled the air.

Colonel Halverson's full report of Kegham's actions earned him the Silver Star. One month later at GHQ, eleven wounded cannoneers of Company D, some standing and some in wheelchairs, faced General Pershing. The General went down the line pinning on their Purple Heart medals. Kegham straightened up in his wheelchair, making an effort to salute, but General

Pershing's hand gently stopped the attempt. "Congratulations, Private Agegian, for risking your life to save the lives of two of your fellow soldiers. This medal will always be a reminder of your heroic act."

"Thank you, Sir. They would have done the same for me."

"I'm sure they would have," assured General Pershing.

The general went on to wish them a safe trip home and was about to turn when Colonel Halverson stepped closer. "Sir, there's one more member of Company D – Second Lieutenant Shaw."

General Pershing pondered – had he missed someone? Colonel Halverson leaned closer and, with a gleam in his eye, whispered, "Bullshit, sir."

The Commander-in-Chief moved briskly to where Fred was standing. But before Fred could salute, General Pershing extended his hand. As they shook hands, the C-in-C flashed a broad smile. "It's an honor and a pleasure to meet you, Lieutenant Shaw."

The Kentucky farm boy saluted and responded, "Likewise, Sir, and that's no bull." If the brother's pride could glow, it would have blinded everyone within 100 yards.

The war continued several more agonizing months. On Nov. 11, 1918, in a railway car on a siding in a French forest, the representatives from both sides signed the documents bringing peace to a war-weary world. It was heralded as "the war to end all wars," but world events had their own agenda for the next generation.

After the war, America emerged as a world power. Its industrial strength and scientific achievements would carry her into the remainder of the 20th century and beyond as the unchallenged leader in the world community of nations.

Early in the 19th century, General Simón Bolivar, "the Liberator" of South America, while visiting New York City was asked by a reporter what he thought of their country. His answer had the full force of prophetic accuracy. "America is not a country. It is an assignment of destiny."

45

Brothers Never Forget

Kegham tried to position himself in bed as much as his injury would allow. "Dear Mother and Father"—no, "Dear Mom and Dad." As he wrote the revised greeting, he paused and looked down the ward at the neatly aligned rows of white metal beds filled with soldiers, each with his own personal story of survival. As he pondered the scene, the swinging double doors of the ward flew open. A beaming Nick, pushing Bob's wheelchair, raced down the center aisle as fast as the speed limit would allow, followed by Fred and Bill, carrying enough flowers to start a wholesale flower business, singing "over hill, over dale…" They surrounded Kegham unceremoniously dumping the flowers all over his bed. The brothers restrained themselves from embracing their brother with too much gusto, careful not to cause unnecessary pain.

The outburst of applause and whistles from the other beds reached the nurses' station. In seconds, the head nurse, followed by several other nurses, entered the ward, but only for a brief moment and quickly left without being noticed. The therapeutic effect of joy is one medicine injured soldiers can't get enough of. The five brothers reminisced until the end of visiting hours was announced. No one was about to resist the wishes of an angel.

As the lights went out and the last bits of conversation faded away, the door opened and a tender voice flowed through the ward, "Good night, boys."

As if on cue, the responses followed, "Good night, Mommy."

"Would you please tuck me in?"

"Don't I get a good night kiss?"

"I'm afraid of the dark - honest."

"Sleep tight, children. Mommy loves all of you." The doors swung back and forth a few times and stopped. Slowly, a soothing calm settled over the darkened ward soon to be punctuated with the sounds of nasal nocturnes from unknown composers.

Kegham lay in bed covered with flowers, the happy voices of his brothers still in his ears. He stared up at the high ceiling and soon was magically transferred to 349 Elm Street. It was the last thing he remembered before falling asleep. In a few weeks, Nick, Bob, and Kegham were on a troop ship homeward bound. Fred and Bill remained behind until the end of the war and then were assigned occupation duties in Germany until 1919.

46

"Home Sweet Home"

A month later, Kegham was discharged from an army hospital in Maryland and with his bulging duffle bag, boarded the train for Watertown. The mental picture of the narrow pathway leading to the porch of 349 Elm Street was clear in every detail. It was over a year since he had last seen his parents. He didn't write the date of his homecoming because he reveled in surprises.

Next stop: Watertown—perfect timing for dinner at home. Anxiety, joy, and anticipation crowded his thoughts. Flashes of Rose scooting around the kitchen baking, cooking, cleaning, talking, and laughing passed by in a series of mind pictures. He was sure he smelled freshly baked *kata*. "Sorry, Dad, I never made general." He quickly suppressed a loud laugh down to a quiet inner chuckle.

The gathering darkness outside had transformed the train's window into a huge mirror. He studied his reflection. He didn't recognize what he saw. Something had changed. He carefully studied his face in the window. The more he looked, the more elusive was the answer to the changes he was seeing.

This much he felt. He was coming back a more mature person. While Kegham's childhood had already given him a head start, the war only added to it. The war had changed the lives of so many young men and Kegham was no exception. The forced maturity that the battlefield stamps on a soldier can either be an asset or a liability.

Rose sat across the kitchen table looking at her brother reading the *Watertown Herald*. The only part of him visible was his big hands holding the paper, and the top of his head. The Regulator clock in the hallway was ticking annoyingly loud.

She focused on the empty third chair and then to the two telegrams from the War Department: one informing them of Kegham's injury and the other of his decoration for bravery. It was taking its toll on Rose—the most devastating was not being with her *anoushik* Kegham.

George tried his best not to compound the prevailing gloom at dinner time by trying to engage his sister in a game of Crazy-Eights, her favorite card game, but with no success.

Rose abruptly pulled the newspaper down and in a plaintive voice said, "Kegham hasn't written in over a month."

George tried to come up with a reasonable answer but was tongue tied. She started crying, barely catching her breath as tears streamed down her cheeks. George resumed reading.

This time, she tore the newspaper from George's hands, leaving pieces in each hand and in

135

a voice choking with anger, she shouted, "How could you sit there reading the comics?!"

"I'm not reading the comics," replied George. "You'd better have plenty of *kata* ready. We'll be hearing from Kegham any day now. Our hero will need to make up for lost time."

George knew the minute he finished that it was the wrong tact. Mother Rose's emotional pain gripped every fiber of her being. Her head dropped on the table, cradled in her muscular arms. Her sobs filled the little house on Elm Street. A frustrated George quietly got up to leave, hoping for some respite from his sister's emotional outbursts. Tomorrow he planned to close the store early for repairs on the sewing machine. "I'll be right back, Rose. There are a few things that need checking."

Rose's mournful voice cried out, "You can keep right on going and don't ever come back." It was an impossible situation.

George was about to unlock the back door to his shop when he noticed a figure carrying a large bag over his shoulder, half walking, half running towards him. *"Der Asdvadz!"* (Lord God)

"Dad, I'm home for good!" Rose's sharp ears heard. Her burley figure charged out of the front door nearly tearing the screen door off of its hinges. All Rose could do was hold her son in her arms. No words, just sobs and hiccups between sobs.

Mother and son hugged all the way into the house with George trailing behind, carrying the "General's" baggage. The little house on Elm Street was coming back to life.

Kegham dropped into his chair. Rose and George joined their son around the table. All they could do was look at each other. Joy had paralyzed their vocal chords. Finally, Kegham broke the silence. "Mom, I haven't eaten since eight this morning." George, trying hard to steady his quivering lower lip, slapped the table. "No more army chow—from now on, it's the best from Chef Rose for our son."

For the next half hour, Rose danced the light fantastic between the stove, ice box, sink and back to the stove. She was in her glory. The single light above the table shone brightly down on three people whose happiness spread into every corner of the house.

Rose said the Lord's Prayer, "*Hayr Mer*," in Armenian, and they began eating, talking and laughing. It was just as if Kegham had never left. Kegham slapped his forehead, "I picked up something at a second hand store." He quickly returned with an old oak frame enclosing the hand embroidered words, "Home Sweet Home." "Where shall we hang it, Mom?" Only silence and tears from George and Rose. Kegham took his chair at the table, sensing the impact the framed words were having on them.

George broke the silence, "When are we to get the best *kata* in the world?" That sent everything into motion again. Rose bounced out of her chair to warm up the *kata*. George gave his trademark wink to Kegham. 349 Elm Street was back to straining its foundations. "Home Sweet Home" and Mom's *kata*.

47

Joan's Repeat Performance

Kegham stayed close to home, reading and visiting friends. He paid Mr. Hardy a visit at Hood Rubber Company. He was warmly welcomed. An offer for employment was politely refused.

Kegham walked through the plant talking with friends and left before the shift ended. His thoughts flashed back two years earlier, remembering an eager, enthusiastic boy running breathlessly, calculating his weekly earnings.

He couldn't stop a short laugh acknowledging that the ways of youthful exuberance no longer had their place. The future was impatiently waiting and it had no place for the simple, carefree reactions of a young boy.

June 16 was a few weeks away and Joan's penchant for planning special events started to germinate. Her letter to Rose laid out the plans for a surprise party for Kegham's 20th birthday.

"Serious mistake, Joan dearie." Rose's letter left little doubt who was going to arrange the party. The Stantons and Thompsons were the honored guests. "Leave the rest to me, Joan. Yours truly, Rose."

Red, white, and blue bunting dominated the church hall. The food was to be prepared in several select homes close to the church, and then delivered to the small church kitchen minutes before the big surprise party.

Every detail of the project was directed from beginning to end and beyond by "Sergeant" Rose. Her troop of ladies followed her instructions without question. They knew how much the party meant to her.

Through the years, Rose had gained the friendship of many parishioners at St. Gregory's. She was a unique woman, never self-absorbed, always friendly and considerate to the needs and wishes of those around her.

Joan, Bob, and the Stantons drove down Thursday and checked into the hotel. They reached the church hall at 7 p.m., and in a few minutes were assigned duties that lasted until 11 p.m., and then another hour to finalize details.

One concession that Joan had wrung out of Rose was the birthday cake. She located a baker whose masterpiece left everyone ooing and ahhhing as two husky men carefully carried in the towering six layered masterpiece, placing it gently on the head table.

Joan had done something that no one expected; a surprise of her own. Preparations were started weeks earlier with a telegram to 2nd Lt. Fred Shaw and Staff Sergeant Bill Stuart in France. Bill's parents in Ohio sent an enlarged photo of the five brothers, their arms around each other on the day they bivouacked outside of Rheims. Bill had arranged for a French photographer to take the picture for a couple of packs of cigarettes. Best of all—a telegram from Bob and Nick. Joan was almost in tears—"Look honey...."

Bob read the telegram, "We'll be in Watertown Station Friday. 4pm. Can't wait to help in the surprise party for our brother Kegham."

Everything was ready to explode with such force that Joan was having anxiety attacks. Bob eased her fears with words of assurance. He looked at his wife with a heart filled with pride. He felt so grateful for that fateful night over six years ago when they first met at the church social in Troy.

Rose checked and rechecked every detail. Tables spaced in perfect order. Plates, cups, forks, spoons, and napkins were all uniformly in place. The 200+ guests began filling the hall. Nick and Bob impatiently waited in a side room, ready to make their appearance on cue. Excitement coupled with tension was rapidly filling the hall. The Big Surprise was only minutes away.

George stretched his arms and eased out of his chair, casually turning to Kegham. "What's keeping your mother? It's nearly seven o'clock. I'm hungry. Let's go to church and see what's keeping her."

Hiding behind a large elm tree, a vigilant young boy waited overflowing with excitement. The front door opened. A resurrected ten-year-old Paul Revere, minus a horse, dashed down the alley, hopping over fences, and bursting into the packed hall. "They're coming!"

Lights went out and excited voices continued talking. A few shushes and 200+ guests held their collective breaths.

An impatient, irritated Rose whispered under her breath, "What's keeping George?" Some sounds outside the hall door.

"There's no one here, Dad" George immediately replied. "Look, the door is open." George was bubbling over with glee. They entered the darkened hall, but what was expected didn't happen. The lights, the shouts of "surprise!"—George's patience ran out quickly. "Where's everybody?"

The lights brought to life the packed hall followed by the ringing sounds of "Surprise!" Kegham stood frozen, unable to move or speak. He was hustled to the main table and seated between George and Rose under a large American flag suspended from the ceiling.

Joan finally got order and began the evening program. Her voice faded away as Kegham sank deep into his past. A multitude of events bombarded his thoughts. So much had happened in three years. His destiny had guided each step flawlessly. Everything seemed to have been planned. Each unfolding of events fit in a pattern that ensured his survival. The more he thought of his journey from Khunoos, the more he felt that it was God's work. It was this belief that would stay with him for the rest of his life.

Joan was approaching the most exciting moments of the evening. "Folks, I have a telegram to read that comes all the way from France."

"Dear Brother Kegham, we send our best wishes on your birthday. We'll always cherish our friendship and salute with pride our brother Kegham. Happy Birthday. God Bless You. Bill Stuart and Fred Shaw, Company D."

The telegram sent waves of previous memories over Kegham. He read the telegram during the applause and neatly folded it and placed it in his shirt pocket. Joan continued, "The other two brothers haven't responded," and feigning deep disappointment, "I don't know why." That was the cue. Bedlam was about to break loose in mere seconds. The door from a side room opened and out popped a glowing Nick and Bob. The sudden, unexpected shock brought Kegham to his feet, sending his chair propelling back against the wall. The brothers crashed in a three-way embrace. The crowd rose from their chairs, applauding and cheering. The noise decibel was fast approaching the point where windows, light bulbs, loose paint, cups, and glasses were in danger of shattering, peeling, or cracking.

The excitement of the opening moments of the festivities rolled on. Friends surrounded Rose and George showering them with well wishes. Rose cried and smiled. George glowed with pride.

Bob turned to his mother-in-law and in a genuinely inquisitive voice asked, "Mom, how did Joan find Kegham's war-time buddies and how did she manage that fabulous cake on such short notice?"

The answer was quick, "Bob, dear, Joan has been a human dynamo from the day she was born." Then Mrs. Stanton added, "Bob, we are so happy that fate brought the two of you together," and leaning over she gave her son-in-law a warm, motherly hug and kiss.

Father Levon waited for the chatter and excitement to show signs of running their course. He tapped his glass a few times, and the crowd responded and took their places.

"I can't imagine the calories that have been burned so far this evening. Don't worry; you won't collapse for lack of nourishment, thanks to Rose's corps of ladies...." Spontaneous applause cut off Father Levon's next words. He patiently waited, then decided it best to go right into the Lord's Prayer.

After the blessing, eager eyes watched the serving ladies disappear into the kitchen. The never-ending stream of food flowed out of the small kitchen. The calorie count merrily climbed with no end in sight.

At 9:00 p.m., Joan invited Kegham to cut his birthday cake. He blew out the candles with ease. Next in order, the guest of honor's eagerly anticipated "birthday speech."

A respectful hush descended over the hall. Every eye was on Kegham. A very serious young man rose and faced a sea of faces. Privately he was drifting into a world filled with the glow of warm and unqualified love. Kegham stood silent for what seemed like eternity. His soul was about to speak. The moment demanded nothing less.

As the last cough and the sounds of clinking coffee cups and spoons faded away, he began, "I have been blessed with the love and generosity from many people in the course of my journey to Amerika. Their images will dwell in my heart forever. I would not be here tonight if it were not for the encouragement and help they gave this young immigrant.

"My mother died giving birth to my sister, Victoria. Our first stepmother passed away shortly due to illness. Our second stepmother…" Kegham stopped and corrected himself—"our second mother was a wonderful woman named Mariam. She brought joy and happiness into our lives." Kegham had to stop—he couldn't find the words. A moment of silence and, after a deep breath, he continued, "My life's journey has brought me to this moment and made it possible to fulfill an emptiness and yearning that has been with me since the day I stood in my father's blood and heard my little brother Setrak's last words—'*Myreek,*

145

Myreek.'" Total breakdown—uncontrolled sobs overcame Kegham. Every face in the hall was streaming with tears; every heart felt his pain. In silence they respectfully waited.

Kegham strained to regain his composure. "I never thought I'd ever say the word '*Myreek*' again. But tonight, I'm the happiest and proudest person in the world. Kegham turned to Rose and George and in a strong steady voice, "I love you, *Myreek*. I love you, *Hyreek*."

Rose cupped her hands over her eyes. Her body trembled and shook with every sob. Kegham kissed her. George was totally lost. He struggled to rise, almost falling back into his chair. Kegham pressed George to his chest in a strong embrace, "I love you, Dad." Everyone started hugging and kissing. The applause gave way to a chorus of 200+ voices singing, "For he's a jolly good fellow...."

A few late-night passersby outside the hall stopped to listen. "What's going on at St. Gregory's? They've got a packed house tonight."

48

When Opportunity Crashes Down Your Door, Don't Sue for Damages

In the years following the war, the brothers all settled down to their life's work. Bob Colombo entered Harvard Law School, specializing in corporate law. Upon graduation, he was offered a position with a New York law firm.

Nick Spiros and his father bought an existing restaurant—remodeled it along with its menu and, after a lot of hard work, it became a landmark Greek restaurant in Newark, New Jersey.

Fred Shaw never left the army and eventually rose to the rank of Colonel. He was killed on Omaha Beach on June 6, 1944, directing landing operations.

Bill Stuart joined the Cleveland Police Department. After a few years of night school classes in police science, he passed the test for detective and went on to become Assistant Chief of Police.

Life for Kegham was beginning to resemble a rudderless boat floating in circles. After breakfast, a few short steps into George's shoe store for half an hour or so and then off to the library. He practically wore out a path to the magazine section. The photos in the *National Geographic* had never left him. The cowboys, Indians, the alligators of Florida, etc.... He was sure his future was somewhere other than Watertown, but where?

The day's routine started as usual, out the front door of 349 Elm Street and through the back door of George's shoe store. This time Kegham picked up the *Watertown Herald* left by a customer and began scanning the pages, finally ending up in the want ad section.

A quarter-page ad caught his eye. The Ford Motor Company of Highland Park, Michigan, was scheduled to hold interviews for the position of Employee Relations Coordinator. The ad continued— applicants must be fluent in another language other than English. Armenian was on the list of a dozen languages. Interviews were scheduled at the Anderson Ford Dealership, Saturday at 9:00 a.m.—"Just two days away!"

As Kegham stepped off the streetcar, he caught sight of a line of applicants in front of the dealership. He recognized several faces from St. Gregory's.

At 9:00 a.m. sharp, the door to the dealership opened. The men filed in and took seats in front of a small table. Kegham's eyes focused on one of the three Model T Fords on the showroom floor. Their black chaises gleamed in the morning light. He enjoyed a brief fantasy moment driving his parents around town, visiting friends.

Mr. Bolton, the Ford representative, introduced himself, thanked the group for responding to the ad, and went directly into his presentation. "The Employee Relations Coordinator is a creation of Mr. Ford. It is the only one of its kind in the automotive manufacturing industry. Its objective is to help immigrant employees to manage their paychecks wisely so as to improve their families' lives by fostering frugality and savings—the two key elements in this program."

He continued, "A good observer can get a fairly good idea if the employee's earnings are being spent wisely by noting any new household items such as sofas, chairs, lamps, rugs, etc. The general condition of the house – is it clean and well-maintained? Always try to make complimentary comments, and if you need to make a suggestion, do it in a nonthreatening and helpful manner. You are a friend—not a snooper or meddler and—oh, yes—if offered food or drink, always politely refuse." Mr. Bolton continued listing other duties: no longer than 30 minutes per visit, forms to be submitted each day, etc. The best part was still to come.

"You'll be on a straight salary of $65 a week. The applicants began to show signs of rapid breathing …$65 a week! Blood pressures were approaching dangerously high levels when Mr. Bolton added, with a smile, "Finally, you'll be making all your calls in a company car, which will be returned to the company garage after each day's visits." It definitely wasn't the time for weak hearts.

Kegham's eyes focused on the Model T Ford in the showroom floor with such intensity that it could have peeled off the paint.

The next and final phase of the interview required each of the language groups to take a short test. They were to translate into English a prepared statement in their own language. If it was satisfactorily translated, they were given a preliminary letter of acceptance, along with a week's training at the Highland Park Plant plus driving lessons courtesy of Mr. Ford.

Kegham tried to contain his exuberance when he heard his name was one of three Armenians selected. The excited selectees filled the showroom with a cacophony of languages. Mr. Bolton interrupted, "Gentlemen—gentlemen." The applicants' enthusiastic responses quickly faded. Kegham was savoring, with charged anticipation, the beginning moments of a great adventure.

Mr. Bolton continued, "This packet will be all the instructions you'll need—read it carefully. If for any reason you should change your mind, please let Mr. Anderson know."

"Thank you and good luck," were Mr. Bolton's parting words.

Kegham bolted out of the dealership. By the time he got off at his streetcar stop, the sobering effect of leaving home began crowding his thoughts. But, somehow, he knew that this was an opportunity that he wasn't going to let slip away.

"Mom and Dad will just have to understand." It wasn't going to be easy to leave the third chair empty a second time. It looked like February 1919 was going to be an exceptionally cold month.

49

The Empty Chair

Rose could always sense whenever Kegham had something of importance to tell them and it always came during dinner time. That evening, Kegham relished every morsel, smiling between helpings. The food never tasted so good.

Rose began her subtle interrogation, "Kegham *hokis*, what did you do today? Go anywhere special?"

Kegham responded without hesitation, "I applied for a job at Anderson's Ford dealership downtown."

George held back his next mouthful, "You're not thinking about selling cars?"

Rose interrupted in defense, "What's wrong with selling cars?"

Kegham began a full accounting of what had transpired. As he related the full scope of the job, what he expected to see, a pair of sad countenances, never happened. To his amazement, his parents were responding with acceptance and even enthusiasm.

All sorts of questions about the interview and who were the other Armenians selected kept Kegham busy answering. Rose's one remark helped to eliminate any anxiety Kegham might have had when she said, "Be very careful driving in Detroit. It's a big city, not like our little Watertown."

George quickly added, "Don't worry, Rose. There won't be any problems our son can't handle." Then, with his trademark wink, "Our Kegham is a quick learner." In a few seconds hot *kata* from the oven, tea, and honey graced the table.

What Kegham thought would be a difficult and stressful event turned out just like any other day. It made it easier to continue talking about his new job.

In all the excitement, he had forgotten to check the packet of instructions. "Folks, I don't know when and where to report." A quick dash to his bedroom left two forlorn souls facing each other.

Rose was fighting back tears. George sent a cautionary signal. She regained her composure and beamed a smile as Kegham returned. Two quick bites of *kata* and he eagerly went through the contents of the packet.

A premature feeling of loneliness was beginning to settle over Rose and George as they watched their son excitedly read the instructions. "Report - 9am, February 20 at 210 Manchester Ave., Room B." Rose and George knew that the contents of that small envelope were going to change life at 349 Elm Street. How much, they weren't quite sure.

February 20 was almost two weeks away, leaving plenty of time to prepare for Detroit's exciting and promising future. So what was there left for loving parents to do but to accept the fact that children sooner or later leave home. One can't live in a vacuum clinging to past joys. Rose and George reluctantly rationalized that what was of paramount importance was Kegham's future which they were ready to support with a never-ending stream of unqualified love.

50

Going in Style

Bob had found his small-town practice in Danville, Vermont. The front room of their rented farmhouse became his consultation office and the hallway the waiting room. Joan applied the full force of her endless supply of energy, receiving and scheduling patient visits. She meticulously kept records on a new upright Underwood typewriter, a gift from her parents.

As Bob's practice grew, so did Joan's involvement. "Thompson Inc." was back in business. It seemed so natural to be working together again. The one-room school house had faded away without a sign of regret from Joan.

Kegham read Joan's letter of congratulations on his new job. The post script brought on a smile— "Kegham dear, my dad will be there next Saturday to give you driving lessons so you can pass without trouble at Ford's." Joan always found ways to arrange matters and anticipate needs.

Saturday afternoon, Edith and Rose sat around the kitchen table talking and eating while the men and Kegham went driving around in circles on the high school playground and the less traveled roads around town. Kegham shifted gears, stopped and backed up. By 6:00 p.m., improvement was clearly visible.

Sunday was graduation day. Mr. Stanton handed the keys to Kegham while George cranked up the car, hopped in, and off they went past St. Gregory's, Hood Rubber Company, and Arsen's restaurant. No one experienced the slightest jolt, jar, or jerk. Mr. Stanton jokingly commented, "Either I'm a terrific teacher or Kegham is a sharp student."

Rose couldn't wait. "You're absolutely right, Bill. My Kegham is a very quick learner."

George filled in what was missing. "Thanks, Mr. Stanton, for taking the time and patience to help our son."

Bill responded, "I don't dare disobey Captain Joan's orders."

Monday morning, Rose went on a buying spree. Kegham's pleas had no effect. In a few hours, she had purchased a three-piece suit, with extra pants, five shirts, five ties, five pairs of socks, and five BVDs. She was contemplating the magic number ten had not Kegham's pleas brought her back to reality. Rose got the last word, two sweaters and one overcoat.

Departure day was the following Wednesday. Tuesday night, Rose started packing the suitcase. She had to sit on it while Kegham tightened the straps. "Mom, if you were 30 pounds lighter, we'd never have closed this suitcase." This changed the sadness building up in Rose into a hearty laugh. She hugged her son in an unexpected tender embrace, the meaning of which did not go unnoticed by Kegham.

The three residents of 349 Elm Street, that fate had brought together, walked past St. Gregory's to the streetcar stop at 4th and Johnson. As they waited, a deep melancholy enveloped Kegham. The memory of an immigrant boy stepping off the streetcar at the same stop just a few years earlier crowded into his thoughts. It was a moment of joy and sadness intertwined.

Kegham helped his mom up the high steps of the streetcar. His dad followed with the bulging suitcase. The conductor stepped on the floor bell— clang! clang! The doors closed and the streetcar rolled towards the train station to a future filled with the promise of a great new adventure.

51

Hello, Detroit

The train pulled into Michigan Central Station at 9 p.m., right on schedule. The Watertown YMCA supplied Kegham with the address of the downtown YMCA in Detroit. "22 Grand Circus Park, please." The cabbie turned the meter handle and Kegham settled back taking in the sights on Woodward Avenue, the premier thoroughfare running almost north and south, dividing the city.

In 1701, *détroit*, the French word for straits, was a small French fur-trading post where the Ojibwe, Algonquin, Huron, and Mohawk came to trade furs for the white man's manufactured products. Now, over two centuries later, Detroit was fast becoming the automobile manufacturing center of the United States, and since 1915, the home of the largest automobile assembly plant in the world. Its sole owner, Henry Ford, had never finished grade school. Where else but in America!

The YMCA room was clean and comfortable. The room clerk assured Kegham that the Ford Highland Park Plant was a short streetcar ride and no transfers would be needed.

Kegham was up early Thursday for some sight-seeing. The Main Library, and just across the street, the Metropolitan Museum, were within easy walking distance. South on Woodward Avenue; a short walk to the Detroit River then a short ferry ride across to Windsor, Canada.

Big lake freighters, their hulls low in the water with the weight of the iron ore from Michigan's Upper Peninsula and Duluth, Minnesota, slowly moved down river towards US Steel's hungry furnaces in Pittsburg.

That night, Kegham concentrated on the ceiling, his favorite evening exercise. The mental images unraveled without effort, like a silent movie. Many replays of 349 Elm Street, with all its joy and the unforgettable moments of love. If home is where the heart is, Kegham had never left home.

"Up at 6:30—no, 6—leave by 7—short ride, no transfers—." The inevitable crept over his senses and Kegham soon succumbed to the sounds of serene slumber. "Tomorrow—tomorrow."

The orientation sessions went without trouble. On the fourth day, he passed the driver's test. "Thank you, Joan—thank you, Mr. Stanton—thank you, Mr. Ford—God Bless Amerika!"

Once a week, a four- or five-page letter from Kegham. Rose read while George listened, "Dear Mom and Dad"—the week's events followed in detail. "I visited four families today. The Karagozians got a high rating. You won't believe it, Mom, but she was baking *kata* at the time of my first visit. Even though we're not supposed to accept food, I had tea and *kata* for the remainder of my stay."

"They're a hard working family and they know how to save and spend wisely…I can drive the Model T almost with my eyes shut…hugs and kisses. Your loving son, Kegham. P.S. Mom, your *kata* is still the best."

Rose pressed the letter to her heart and sent a broad smile towards George, who was concentrating on Kegham's empty chair, wrapped up in his own thoughts. One of Rose's lady friends had mentioned that her sister lived in Highland Park and might have a room to rent. Immediately, a letter with all the particulars was in the mail.

Kegham stood in front of the two-story brick house at 119 Labelle Avenue. A satisfied smile was for the short 20 minutes it took to walk from Ford's—"So far, so good."

The doorbell was answered by a pleasant lady, "Come in Kegham. We've been expecting you."

A few minutes of the usual pleasantries, and both parties agreed to $45 a month for room and board. His bedroom was spacious, with two opposing windows, plus a private outside staircase. More satisfied smiles beamed from Kegham.

In the ensuing weeks, Siranoush Kevorkian found great pleasure in surprising Kegham with special Armenian dishes. A laugh, bordering on a plea, from her husband, Mihran, as he jokingly remarked, "Please stay as long as you like, so I can enjoy my wife's treats—in fact, you can stay for free." Lots of laughter—just like at the little house on Elm Street.

Once a week, the unmistakable box filled with neatly packed *kata*, would be waiting on the dining room table. The Kevorkians were also waiting for the package from 349 Elm Street. It was *kata* and tea that night—just like home. "Thanks, Mom."

It wasn't long before Kegham's National Bank of Detroit savings book's last entry showed a hefty $487 balance. "How am I doing, Mr. Ford?" Everything in dynamic Detroit was going in the right direction for the soon-to-be 21-year-old young man. If there was a smile meter, it would have sprung its springs by now. "God Bless Amerika!"

52

Myreek!

At first, the empty third chair had not seriously impacted the residents at 349 Elm Street. But as the days stretched into weeks, the emptiness that Kegham had filled was returning in full force.

Rose made several trips to Detroit. George was able to accompany her on one of them. After a while, the visits lessened. Kegham went home on few weekends, but it proved impractical.

One day, Rose started developing a persistent cough. Joint pains were next. Her energy was being affected. She was growing listless and neglecting her household chores. Father Levon's knock was not answered. He went next door, "George, where is Rose?"

"She's home, Father," replied George. They both rushed into the house. Rose lay in bed, pale and perspiring, and, in a weakened voice, whispered, "I'm not feeling well, George."

Father Levon and George helped Rose out of the taxi at the emergency entrance of St. Vincent Hospital. An orderly wheeled her to the emergency room. She was already coughing traces of blood. George phoned Dr. Bob from the hospital. "Dr. Bob, please come. Rose is very sick." George's sobbing voice could barely finish without crying.

"I'll be there tomorrow, George. Don't worry; she's going to be okay."

Dr. Bob rushed to the reception desk and in minutes was in consultation with the attending physician. Joan, George, and Father Levon sat waiting in the reception room. Father Levon silently prayed. George bent over and buried his face in his hands. Sadness was etched all over Joan's face.

The minutes dragged on. A sober Dr. Bob returned. "Rose has a severe case of the Spanish Flu virus, one of the few remaining cases in Massachusetts. She has to be kept in isolation." George silently stared at the floor. His life was being swept into a premature loneliness.

Mrs. Kevorkian was waiting in the hallway holding a telegram from Joan. Her facial expression wiped away Kegham's greeting smile. "What's the matter, Mrs. Kevorkian?" She hoped it was not bad news.

Kegham read and cried out a shrill, "*Myreek*! *Myreek*!" The promises for Detroit had just collapsed. Nothing mattered except to get home to his mother's side.

53

Never to Be

Kegham's tragic past was always waiting on the sidelines ready to surface in full force. In a frantic, barely audible voice, he spoke to himself, "I need to go home." Before Mrs. Kevorkian could respond, the front door closed behind Kegham. The homes on Labelle Avenue flashed by in a blur.

Mr. Bolton faced a perspiring employee, whose pitiful voice was grasping for words. "Mr. Bolton, my *myreek*...my mother, is very sick. She's in the hospital...I have to leave right away. I came to tell you...I..."

Mr. Bolton responded without hesitation, "I understand, Mr. Agegian. Don't worry about anything. Stay as long as necessary. Don't worry about this end."

The calm, reassuring words were enough to fill Kegham's eyes with tears. He grasped Mr. Bolton's hand, "Thank you, Sir. Thank you, thank you."

Mr. Bolton went one step further and drove Kegham to the train station. He noted that no time for preparations had been taken. Before Kegham could get out of the car, Mr. Bolton slipped some money into Kegham's coat pocket, "Just in case." Kegham rushed out of the car, then caught himself. "God bless you, Mr. Bolton."

George and Joan sat staring at the floor.
George remembered his sister's weakened voice on the
way to the hospital, "George, no need to worry our
Kegham. We can explain everything after I'm better.
You know there's a lot of *kata* to be mailed to my
anoushik." Sharp sparks of pain pierced George's
heart. He closed his eyes and suffered in silence.

A weary, disheveled Kegham rushed to the
reception desk. He failed to notice George, Joan, and
Dr. Bob seated in the corner of the reception room.
They rushed to greet him. Bob explained that Rose
was placed in isolation and couldn't be seen. Joan
tenderly led Kegham back to the couch. No one
noticed the four forlorn souls sitting silently waiting.

Nurses in clean, white, starched uniforms,
white shoes, and white stockings silently glided by
seemingly oblivious to anything but their duties. It
was six a.m., the beginning of another work day at St.
Vincent's Hospital.

The next four days saw a steady deterioration
of Rose's condition. The flu virus was consuming the
last vestiges of her once vital force and with it the will
to live.

Orthodox medicine had very little to offer in
the battle against the deadly flu virus that was
estimated to have killed 50 million people worldwide
between 1918-1919. The reports of a 90% success rate
for those treated homeopathically somehow never
reached the newspapers.

Their vigil came to an end at 4 a.m., Saturday. "She has just passed away, Dr. Thompson," the attending doctor discreetly whispered to his fellow physician.

"Thank you, Dr. Williams, for everything you tried to do for Rose." Bob couldn't move. He saw a young boy standing next to the lifeless body of his father, staring into space. Kegham's accumulated life's tragedies crept into Dr. Bob's thoughts. He slowly made his way down the long hallway, and as he turned the corner into the waiting room, his expression left no doubt as to what had happened.

George and Kegham buried their faces in their hands weeping uncontrollably. Joan cried out, "Bob no!"

Bob struggled to speak, "I'm so very sorry," then lost his voice.

Kegham buried his head in George's shoulder and cried over and over, "*Myreek, Myreek, Myreek....*" This time the nurses took notice.

54

Engulfed in Emptiness

Saint Gregory's Armenian Apostolic Church overflowed with Rose's life-long friends and acquaintances. It was standing room only, from the packed pews, the crammed aisles, all the way past the jammed entrance, overflowing down onto the sidewalks. Several times during the services, Father Levon had to pause to regain his composure and wipe away tears.

At the cemetery, uncontrolled emotions left Kegham prostrate on the mound of freshly dug earth. His anguish-filled voice, weighed down with sorrow, pleaded, "*Myreek…Myreek…*I need you. I want you back." A weary George and several pall bearers lifted a limp Kegham and supported him throughout the burial service.

The grave is a finality that is deaf to the pleas and lamentations of the living. Death's only concession is the thin thread of memories for the bereaved, which will in time, inevitably give way to the daily demands of their lives.

The church services, the burial, the traditional memorial dinner, plus the steady stream of condolences, were having their effect on George and Kegham.

That night, the single kitchen light shone on two forlorn, lonely souls sitting around the table in the grip of an unbearable, agonizing silence. Rose's vacant chair spoke in countless bittersweet ways of the days and nights filled with joy and merriment now gone forever. The Regulator clock in the hallway ticked its own sorrowful farewell. The little house at 349 Elm Street was never to rock on its foundation again.

Around 10 p.m., a knock on the screen door broke the silence. George peered through the screen trying to identify the late-night visitor. A gentle voice spoke, "George, it's me, Nellie. I know it's late, but may I please come in?"

George extended his hand, "Please do, Nellie." Nellie sat in Rose's chair. Kegham excused himself and went to his bedroom. He slumped into bed. The familiar ceiling looked down on him but his eyes wouldn't stay opened. His mind was drained and empty like the little house at 349 Elm Street. The muffled sounds of conversation from the kitchen faded as he fell into an uneasy sleep.

Through the years, Nellie and George had exchanged greetings after church, during church socials, but best of all was when George would place newspaper under her feet while Nellie sat waiting for her shoes to be repaired. Nellie had secret thoughts of being part of George's life but never made any overtures in that direction. Nellie Tarpinian was an intelligent, graceful and educated woman in her mid-forties. For over 20 years, she was the chief law clerk at Moriarity, Jones and Alexanian, a highly respected law firm in Watertown.

Something inexplicable had happened for Nellie to make such a bold move late at night and so contrary to her reserved nature. "George, if you and Kegham need anything, please don't hesitate to call me."

George looked into a sincere, compassionate face, "You're very kind and thoughtful, Nellie. We can't thank you enough." At that moment, two hearts began beating the unmistakable message of deep affection.

55

Unfoldings Abound

In the days following the late-night visit, Nellie became a frequent visitor at 349 Elm Street. Her presence began stirring feelings that George never knew existed.

A strong sense of compatibility was growing with each encounter. They went to the theater to watch Charlie Chaplin's antics on the silent screen—evening walks in Prospect Park—dinner at Arsen's Restaurant, and intimate discussions about life in general. There was little doubt that George and Nellie were falling in love.

On the nights they were enjoying each other's company, Kegham was alone in the grip of Rose's voice echoing throughout the house, but the most devastating loss was her unqualified mother's love that had been so cruelly taken away. A cold bitterness fed by a growing sense of despair was settling over Kegham's gentle, optimistic nature. The beginnings of a morbid downward spiral were gathering momentum.

A hasty decision and Kegham boarded the train for Danville, Vermont. Joan set the table and the trio sat down for dinner. Joan glanced at Bob and then to a somber, silent Kegham, whose eyes were saying, "Help me!"

Bob took the lead, "Joan, remember Kegham's first birthday?"

"Oh, how could I ever forget," came Joan's enthusiastic response.

Bob continued, "You can't imagine how hard I tried to keep the temperature in that clay oven constant. I should have taken up baking instead of medicine." Bob and Joan managed a weak laugh.

Bob changed the subject. "When are you heading back to Detroit?"

"Never," was Kegham's immediate response. The Thompson's task was cut out for the rest of the evening.

Joan's unemotional, straight-forward advice was to the point. "Don't let Rose's death jeopardize any decisions concerning your future," then pointedly adding, "Rose would be heart-broken if she could see you now."

Kegham's eyes started to bulge with tears. He hung his head in submission. Between muffled sobs, words surfaced from the depths of his being, "I'm destined never to have a mother's love."

Joan desperately searched for words to counter Kegham's negative mindset. Then her eyes opened wide, followed with a big smile—she had found the right approach. She remembered a few weeks earlier during the funeral, how much she had enjoyed talking to Nellie. Even though it was just a short visit, Joan was impressed. "Look, Kegham; George lost his one and only sister whom he dearly loved, but look what has happened. Nellie has come into his life. It's all very natural and normal."

An inspired Joan continued, "Review your life." Her voice was clear and confident. "You have proven your ability to overcome tragedy and sadness the likes of which few people experience. You were strong as a boy and now even stronger as a man—don't let your drive to survive weaken. We love you very much—never forget that."

Simultaneously, Bob and Joan embraced the charter member of "Thompson Inc." What else could partners do!

The scourge of self-pity was beginning to lose its hold. The love of family he had been seeking all of his life was still possible. The rest of the evening gave way to reminiscing and remembering. Reviving past events was therapeutic for everyone.

Kegham and Brother Fred

Left to right (standing): Turfanda, Kegham, Hazel, Martin, Krikor (seated)

Kegham and Hazel
1923

Volunteer Red Cross Nurses
Hazel (2nd from left)

"Batchelors All"
Kegham (standing, 1st from left)

Kegham's first business venture

Krikor in front of his shoe repair store

*First Lieutenant Martin (standing, 1st from left) and his B-17 "Flying Fortress" crew
1944*

56

Love at First Sight

A relaxed Kegham entered 119 Labelle Avenue just as the Kevorkians were finishing dinner. Siranoush saw a noticeable change in her young boarder. He was calm and in control, quite a change from the day he left.

An extra plate was served for a famished Kegham. They talked about his trip to Watertown. "That sure hit the spot, Mrs. Kevorkian."

"It's good to have you back," added Mihran. Kegham excused himself and went up to his room.

While undressing, he remembered the kindness Mr. Bolton had shown to a panic-stricken employee barging into his office. Recalling the incident was momentarily embarrassing. Tomorrow was a workday, and he was ready to go on with his life.

Kegham remembered when George hugged him at the train station, saying, "You will always be my General, and 349 Elm will always be your home."

Nellie embraced Kegham adding, "I have Rose's *kata* recipe. So don't be surprised when you get a box of *kata* one of these days." Kegham waved from the train as he had done so many times on so many occasions. A smiling George and Nellie waved back. George had his arm around Nellie—how things had changed. A brief moment of longing for the days at 349 Elm Street crept into his thoughts.

By 1921, practically every automobile manufactured in the US was made in Detroit, Michigan. Ford's Model T's came in only one color – black. It swerved, slid, and bounced over all manner of roads in any weather. The growing network of highways couldn't keep up with the assembly lines in Detroit.

Henry Ford's vision of the assembly line made cars affordable even to the workers assembling them. A great economic boom was gathering momentum. Kegham's savings book was filling with lines of deposits. The last entry boosted the astronomical total to $2,357. Watertown had lost its chance. It was now Detroit's honor having the first Armenian-American millionaire. "Thank you, Mr. Ford. God Bless Amerika."

Every October, the Social Democrat Hunchakian Party held its annual *Hunchook* (festival). Music, dancing, homemade food and more, and it didn't matter to which political party you belonged. The second floor hall above the Woolworth store was filled beyond the fire department regulations. No one counted heads—no one cared. People ate, played cards, and backgammon boards clicked with the sound of dice. Kids darted around, playing tag, or sliding on corduroy knickers over polished wood floors.

A five-piece band alternated between American and Armenian music. It was nonstop dancing, eating, and merrymaking.

At the last minute, Kegham and his friends changed direction and instead of going to the movies, they found themselves pushing their way up the packed stairway leading to the hall. The food counters drew his friends, but Kegham looked for an empty chair.

Just as he was about to sit, he spotted an attractive girl a few tables away, sitting next to an older woman and a young boy. He sat staring, making every effort not to draw attention. He couldn't keep his eyes off of her. Up to now, young ladies had never been a serious part of Kegham's life, but something was happening.

In 1922, the road to romance and marriage was full of obstacles for young Armenian men. The traditions carried over from the old country hadn't succumbed to the American way—yet.

A suitor had to be properly introduced to the girl's father. Many a potential son-in-law never got past the first visit. The interrogation was brutal—family background, education, job, earnings, health, etc. A police detective, no matter how experienced, would be about halfway through "Interrogation 101" and with just a few more minutes in the parlor with the girl's father, he would have his Master's degree in cross examination.

The mother also had a part in the process. She would sit out of the line of view of the "victim," thus giving her the advantage of observing and scrutinizing his dress, hand movements, demeanor, and if he turned to look at her, it would be a sign of discourtesy towards the father—definitely a bad move.

The whole process was to discourage any young upstart and it worked. Those weak of will never made it. Oh yes, the young lady in question was sequestered in another room, straining her ears, hoping to catch a word or two of the drama unfolding in the parlor.

As fate would have it, who showed up to talk to the older woman was none other than little Antranik Kuezian, whose parents' home was on Kegham's visitation list. Reaction was quick. Kegham discreetly followed the boy to his parents' table.

Harry and Araxy Kuezian were pleasantly surprised to see Kegham. Before any greetings, Kegham started, "Mrs. Kuezian, do you happen to know the name of that girl sitting over…there?" She was nowhere in sight. "Antranik, I saw you talking to an older woman just a few minutes ago."

"You mean Turfan--I mean, Mrs. Mardirosian? Hazel's little brother, Martin, is my best friend."

It didn't take long for Mrs. Kuezian to recognize the first stages of a love-struck young man. She gave her husband a sweet smile that had but one

176

message, "get on with it, you know what he wants to know."

Harry responded on cue, "Oh, that's the Mardirosians. Her father, Krikor, has a small shoe repair shop on Labelle Avenue. They live at 241 Buena Vista."

George's shoe store in Watertown zoomed by. Kegham's heart started the telltale thumping...the Mardirosians' home was just a short walk away from 119 Labelle Avenue! Kegham was perspiring. It was becoming visibly embarrassing. He awkwardly excused himself and rushed off looking for his friends.

Harry Kuezian enjoyed a quiet chuckle. Araxy was already planning. For the next two weeks, Kegham took nightly walks past the Mardirosians' flat. The courage it took to earn the Silver Star was child's play compared to what he was facing. The anxiety meter needle was heading for the red zone, non-stop.

Araxy had always looked forward to Kegham's visits. He was always courteous and helpful—so why shouldn't a nice Armenian boy have some assistance in matters of the heart?

The Mardirosian and Kuezian families had a long-standing tradition of alternating Saturday night dinners. Each Saturday morning, Turfanda and Araxy would walk to Aram Ohanesian's Royal Market to fill their weekend shopping list.

Royal Market had the freshest vegetables the choicest cuts of lamb and beef; barrels of bulk grains and dried legumes lined the walls like sentinels. The deli counter left nothing to the imagination. Customers were at the mercy of enticing odors that dazzled the olfactory nerves. If smells could be digested, a full meal could be had just by inhaling. On especially big orders, Mr. Ohanesian had truck delivery service. He was years ahead of the times.

This particular Saturday, Araxy invited the Mardirosians to dinner, but Turfanda reminded her that it was the Kuezians' turn to come to dinner. Araxy quickly responded, "You're right, Turfanda, but friends don't keep score on whose turn it is. If it will make you feel better, we'll come two Saturdays in a row." They enjoyed a good laugh and continued shopping.

Once home, Araxy dispatched Antranik to get Kegham. "*Tzakus karus* (my little lambkin), it's very important that you get Kegham as fast as possible."

"Yes, Mama." Antranik was off on a special mission. He was part of something big and important. His little legs churned the air as he raced towards 119 Labelle Avenue just a few blocks away.

In less than twenty minutes, Kegham was in the Kuezian parlor wiping away beads of perspiration. Mr. Kuezian tried hard not to see humor in an anxious and nervous young man sitting stiff as a board on the sofa. "Calm down, it won't be the last time you'll try to convince a young lady that you're the answer to all her prayers," were Harry's welcoming words followed with rolls of laughter. Cold chills swept over poor Kegham.

Mrs. Kuezian interrupted with a tinge of reproach in her voice, "Harry, you're not helping matters with those remarks. I remember you were rolling in perspiration the first time you met my parents." Kegham felt some relief.

Harry continued, "Kegham, my boy, remember one very important thing—women have an uncanny ability to remember insignificant details. We men only deal with important issues." He gave his wife a look that said—"end of conversation."

The Mardirosian family arrived exactly at 6:00. Lo and behold! Who was this gawking young man?

Harry introduced Kegham with such high praise that it sent the perspiration gauge close to flood level.

With dinner finished and the last slice of baklava washed down with coffee, the men moved to the parlor while the ladies cleared the dishes, disappearing into the kitchen. Antranik and Martin started for the front door. The sounds of children playing "kick the can" were an invitation to join. Martin's father gave a stern reminder, "Stay in front of the house."

"Yes, Papa," answered Martin. Kegham noted a gentle-natured, ten-year-old boy.

Mr. Kuezian placed the *tavloo* (backgammon) board on a small table and, in his extroverted, friendly manner, said, "After I trounce Krikor, you're next." Hazel's father looked straight at Kegham, who barely managed a weak smile.

The pressure was building and he had yet to speak a complete sentence to Hazel's father. Kegham hoped Mr. Kuezian would win every game. The games continued unabated; not once did the players notice the silent young man watching every toss of the dice.

After the "good-nights" were exchanged, the guests started for their respective homes, but to the Mardirosians' surprise, Kegham was walking in the same direction.

Some bits and pieces of conversation and Kegham bid them good night and turned the next corner for home. Kegham's feet felt like they had sprouted wings. He effortlessly flew up the outside stairs to his room.

The unfolding of events was multiplying exponentially. A letter and package from Watertown was waiting on his bed. He started to open the package, but sure of its contents, decided to read the letter first.

Father Levon had married George and Nellie in a private ceremony. Nellie's parents and the members of the law firm were the only ones present.

After his first bite of Nellie's *kata*, Kegham relaxed on his bed. On the ceiling, a beautiful Hazel in a white, flowing wedding dress was smiling down at him. He ate two more slices of *kata*. The words came automatically without effort—"*Myreek*, no one can make *kata* like you." Moonlight filtered through the curtains, filling the room with soothing shadows. It had been a full day—sleep came easily. "Tomorrow—tomorrow…why, it's Sunday! See you Monday, Mr. Ford."

57

The Plan

Kegham's first stop Monday morning was the Kuezian home. The company Model T came to an abrupt stop. He made the first three steps in one leap and rang the doorbell, all in one move. As soon as Araxy opened the door she became the target of an enthusiastic hug. It wasn't difficult to figure the reason for this unexpected visit.

The two conspirators chattered like competing magpies. Kegham alternated between interrupting and apologizing. At one point, Araxy suggested, "I think your next move should be to visit Krikor's shoe store. Have your shoes repaired or shined. Tell him about your job, but don't talk too long. Remember, he's a very stern man, and easily annoyed, but don't let that discourage you." Kegham attentively listened to every word.

The visit was short. Mrs. Kuezian got a quick goodbye and Kegham hurried off to work. There had been many happy moments in his life, but this time it was uniquely different. The past was being outdistanced by a rapidly moving present. "General" Kegham was in full command, ready to respond to the unfolding of events that lay ahead.

Kegham made several visits to the shoe store. The visits were short and business like. He was just another customer—but not quite. Mr. Mardirosian was watching and scrutinizing him very carefully.

One Saturday, Kegham decided to pay a visit to the Royal Market, hoping to meet Araxy and Turfanda--and hopefully Hazel--"by accident." It happened, but without Hazel. Mrs. Mardirosian was too alert to think that the sudden appearance of Kegham was a mere coincidence. "Is this your first visit?" she queried.

Araxy immediately came to the rescue. "You must be shopping for your landlady."

A relieved Kegham responded, "Yes, Mrs. Kevorkian needed a few items for tonight's dinner." Araxy gave Kegham a reassuring smile as the two ladies continued down the aisle.

Kegham moved on to fill his non-existent shopping list. "What has one to do to begin a courtship?" Once outside, he decided to pay a visit to the shoe store, albeit from across the street. The plan was to be subtle in exposure but determined in effort.

That night, the ceiling became the setting of detailed fantasies that Kegham had no trouble conjuring up—there was Hazel's mother setting the dinner table and her father full of smiles directed towards the guest of honor. It was during moments like this that sleep came effortlessly.

The following Saturday while shopping, Turfanda reminded Araxy that it was her turn to come for dinner. Araxy agonized all the way to the cashier counter when relief finally came. "Do you think that young man..." Araxy's quick response cut Turfanda off—"You mean Kegham? He would be delighted to accept your invitation."

Turfanda's startled look gave way to hearty laughs from both ladies. Turfanda continued, "Does he have a favorite food?"

"Without a doubt, it's *kata*," came Araxy's quick reply.

Araxy rushed home. "Antranik, go get Kegham, and don't come back without him. Hurry, Tzakus."

Antranik's agile mind didn't need further explanation. He ran out the front door singing, "Here comes the bride...."

"Shame on you, Antranik!" came his mother's mild reprimand. She went to the back porch where Harry was relaxing. "Get ready; we're going to dinner at the Mardirosians'."

"Who??? Mardirosians? Do I know them?" His remarks helped to ease her anxiety.

Antranik covered the five blocks in record time. Mrs. Kevorkian was surprised to see a breathless Antranik. "I've come to take Kegham home with me. We're going to dinner at the Mardirosians' at six o'clock." Kegham recognized Antranik's voice and came down from his room.

Siranoush turned to Kegham. "You're invited for dinner at the Mardirosians'."

"Hurry, we haven't got much time," insisted Antranik.

Mrs. Kevorkian took charge. "Kegham, your dark blue suit—bring it to me and a clean shirt and your favorite red tie."

A fast-moving iron put the final touches on the suit coat and pants. A sprinkle of water and the iron produced a wrinkle-free shirt. Mrs. Kevorkian admiringly said, "You look just like a Ford Company executive."

Kegham started to hug her, but all he could say was a hurried "thanks". Antranik was pulling him towards the door. Mrs. Kevorkian waved, "Have a good time, Kegham!"

58

Motivation Flexes Its Muscles

An excited Antranik scampered up the front porch stairs and impatiently pressed the doorbell. Araxy turned to Kegham, "Our son just can't wait to see Martin. They've been friends since kindergarten." The upstairs buzzer responded.

In seconds Antranik reached Turfanda at the top of the staircase. "Hi, Auntie Turfanda."

"Hello, Antranik." Martin was waiting. The two boys disappeared into the back of the flat.

Hazel took a few steps down to greet Harry and Araxy with hugs. Two stairs lower stood a tense Kegham. His feet seemed to be stuck to the stair. "Hello, Kegham. I'm glad you were able to come," was Hazel's cheerful greeting.

All "General" Kegham could muster was an anemic "Hello." (Her name is HAZEL—stupid!) Sweat glands were activating the pores and perspiration started flooding the body landscape.

Soon, the guests were seated around the dining room table, ready for the Saturday night dinner ritual, indulging in the mouth-watering array of Turfanda's Armenian dishes. Okra stew, bulgur (cracked wheat) pilaf, cheese *burag* (hand-rolled layers of thin dough filled with cheese) baked golden crisp, mixed salad, *yaprak sarma* (ground lamb mixed with rice and spices wrapped in tender grape leaves, then cooked in vegetable broth), *jajuk* (yogurt with chopped cucumbers and garlic), baklava (40 layers of hand-rolled, paper-thin dough with honey-coated walnuts between every 10th layer and then baked to a crisp, light brown), and if that wasn't enough, *kata*!

The table was humming with talk between mouthfuls of food. Kegham's mind drifted to Joan's words, so clear and penetrating. George's love for his sister was still alive. The power of that love was now being directed towards Nellie.

Hazel's smiling face brought Kegham back to the table. He smiled back right by her father's stern scrutiny.

The evening was drawing to a close. Kegham played the winner of the backgammon rematch—Hazel's father—and thankfully lost all three games.

11 p.m.: Time to head for home. "Good night, Kegham."

"Good night, Hazel." (That was a lot better.)

Once outside, Araxy's happy nature wasn't going to be restrained. "Kegham, Turfanda and Hazel really like you."

Harry added, "Score one for our hero."

"I can't thank you enough, Mrs. Kuezian, for all you have done for me."

"You're a good man, Kegham, and deserve a chance for a happy life."

Antranik started, "Here comes the…" but a twisted ear lobe silenced the self-designated cupid. Harry enjoyed the moment, chuckling to himself.

At the next street corner, they parted. Kegham continued on to 119 Labelle Ave. without touching the sidewalk or the steps up to his room—happiness has anti-gravity qualities that, at times, can send the body into levitation mode.

That night, the ceiling became a kaleidoscopic panorama of images racing back and forth in fits and starts. Sleep was postponed—it didn't matter—tomorrow was Sunday.

"See you Monday, Mr. Ford—Good night, dear Hazel."

59

Moving Right Along

A letter from Joan! In uncontrolled
excitement, Kegham eagerly tore the envelope open
and part of the letter inside. Nothing but good news!
Bob was scheduled to attend a three-day seminar at
Detroit's Herman Kiefer Hospital the following
weekend. George, Nellie, and Joan were coming with
him. Then Kegham had a sudden flashback, and there
was Brother Fred, and the word was "Bullshit!"?
Kegham roared with laughter, and a revived
confidence took center stage. He reread the letter
several times. True friends form the framework of
one's life, but the family is its foundation.

The approaching train's engine hissed short
bursts of steam and gradually came to a stop—right on
time. Kegham eagerly searched the train windows.
There, squeezed together, were four smiling faces
beaming from the large Pullman car window.

First stop, the Book Cadillac Hotel, and then
off to the Kevorkians' for dinner. Siranoush had
extended an invitation when Kegham had remarked
about their pending visit to Detroit.

The Kevorkians' words of welcome were
drowned out by an excited Kegham—"These are my
two dearest friends, Dr. Bob and Joan Thompson."
Then, turning to George and Nellie, there was a
discernible pause—the absence of Rose distracted his

thoughts. George saw the expression on Kegham's face and immediately took the lead. "I'm George Manoogian, Kegham's American father, and my wife, Nellie."

Nellie handed a gift wrapped box to Mihran. "*Kata* from 349 Elm Street, just for you." By eventide, there was little doubt that they had always been friends.

Siranoush waved from the porch as Mihran prepared to drive his guests to the hotel. Bob kept insisting that it would have been easier to call a cab. Mihran's retort kept the warm and friendly atmosphere alive. "Doctor Bob, you're in for a pleasant shock. My meter is out for repairs—I'll have to charge the flat rate—$100." Kegham and Mihran rode up front, and the two husbands, groaning with laughter, crammed in the back, their wives on their laps, as they headed down Woodward Avenue.

Meanwhile, back at 119 Labelle Avenue, Siranoush was busy planning. "I've got three days before they leave." The plan was quite simple. "The Kuezians and Mardirosians for dinner," she pondered aloud. "We can seat twelve adults using the two extensions for the dining room table and the boys in the kitchen. Children enjoy being alone."

The very first thing tomorrow morning, a quick visit with Araxy.

60

Preparations and Palpitations

"Siranoush, that's a terrific idea," cried out an excited Araxy, still in her bathrobe. How fortunate that Kegham's family and friends were visiting Detroit. In seconds (after a quick change), Araxy headed for the front door. "Let's get to Turfanda's right now." Her exuberance swept Siranoush in its wake.

The two ladies kept a brisk pace all the way to Turfanda's flat. Turfanda's excitement mounted as she listened to the two energized conspirators explain their plan for Saturday night.

Turfanda joined the excitement:, "If Krikor gives me any trouble, he'll spend the next month sleeping on the dirty floor of his store, smelling old rubber heels and worn out leather soles." A three-way pact of steel had just been formed. No other suitor had the support of such powerful forces.

The door of the Royal Market flew open. Turfanda collared Mr. Ohanesian. "I want lamb kabob for 14 people—no grizzle. Start marinating right away." All that was missing was a salute from Mr. Ohanesian.

The ladies' enthusiasm was contagious—"I'll have everything ready. Where shall I deliver?"

"119 Labelle," came Siranoush's response.

"By eight o'clock Saturday," added Araxy.

"No fat, no grizzle," were Turfanda's parting orders. Mr. Ohanesian was still standing at attention after the ladies left.

That night an exuberant Kegham parked the company car, rushed past the guard, and headed for home. The normal 20-minute walk burst into a 10-minute power walk.

Kegham greeted a smiling Siranoush, and then skipped past her, leaping two steps at a time up to his room. A laughing Siranoush shouted, "Kegham, I've got fantastic news to tell you!!!"

"Good news could only have to do with Hazel," was the thought that charged through his brain. With a 180-degree turn and two steps at a time down, he was soon listening to the preparations being made for tomorrow's dinner. It was electrifying. "Did Mrs. Mardirosian really say that about Hazel's father?" They both enjoyed a hearty laugh.

A strong hug from Kegham sent its unmistakable message of appreciation clearer than any well-chosen words. Kegham ran all the way to the street-car line. Catapulting thoughts filled his head— "The world is mine!"

The elevator was too slow—finally the 8th floor. George answered the door and immediately was in a vise-like hug—Kegham's excited, high-pitched voice shouted, "Dad, I'm in love with a wonderful girl." Nellie, Dr. Bob, and Joan bolted from the adjoining room.

"What's going on?" inquired Joan.

"I've met the most wonderful person—I'm going to marry her." George turned toward Nellie with a dazed look. Shock waves were gripping the occupants of the room. One by one, they slumped into the nearest chair...stunned and open-mouthed.

Nellie asked, "What's her name?"

"Hazel...Hazel Mardirosian," came Kegham's words flowing like a swift mountain stream. "You're all invited to a special dinner tomorrow at Mr. and Mrs. Kevorkian's. You'll meet Hazel and her family and the rest of my friends. Oh, Dad, I'm so happy!"

Kegham's one-sided conversation continued all the way down to the hotel dining room and throughout dinner. Finally, the stunned foursome waved their goodbyes to the "groom" as the taxi disappeared in the traffic.

Bob turned to Joan—Joan turned to Nellie—Nellie turned to George—speechless, but in a pleasant state of shock.

Kegham skipped up the outside stairs to his room and leaped into bed. There had been so many tomorrows in his life, but this one was to top them all. The accumulated excitement of the day filled his room, radiating everywhere. He vainly tried to sort out the heavy traffic of thoughts racing through his head. The unfolding of events was multiplying out of control.

If the ceiling had feelings, it would have resented being totally ignored. Kegham kicked off his shoes, rolled over, repeating "tomorrows" until somewhere between the "tomorrows," he fell asleep.

Kegham couldn't believe the hands on the clock—10:30 a.m.—was it exhaustion or was it contentment?—maybe exhausted contentment that caused him to oversleep— and fully dressed!

Meanwhile, downstairs, preparations had been going on since 8:00 a.m. Kegham rushed down. BRIGHT LIGHTS, BEATING DRUMS, TRUMPETS BLARING—there was Hazel!!

Siranoush's voice broke the moment of bliss. "Kegham, tell Mihran to get the two table extensions. He knows where they are."

She was just about to ask Hazel to join the ladies in the kitchen, but caught herself just in time— "Hazel, dear, give Kegham a hand with the chairs." Heaven was about to descend on the dining room. For the next half hour, two happy people kept changing the chairs from one place to another for no other reason than to spend time together.

Tender memories crowded Kegham's heart. "Mom, I wish you were here to see my Hazel."

A lingering emptiness had never left Kegham since the horror filled days in Khunoos. Loving friends, helpful strangers, and George and Rose's generous, unqualified outpouring of parental love only fueled the yearning for that elusive need. The force of a different, more powerful love was about to unmask the phantom that had been haunting him for so long. It was the love of a wife and family of his own that he was seeking. All the reactions to the unfolding of events during Kegham's life were coming together tonight.

Dinner preparations ended around five o'clock. Turfanda and Araxy had already left for home. The charcoal broiler was assembled in the backyard under an old oak tree, waiting for the match to light up the crumpled balls of newspaper neatly placed under rows of charcoal.

The meat had passed Turfanda's close inspection and was in the ice box alongside a 50-pound block of ice. The *kata* dough rose exactly as scheduled and was shaped in eight-inch-round flat shapes, ready for the oven. Low blue flames under cast iron pots were keeping the tempting contents at the correct serving temperature.

Before she left, Turfanda let Hazel stay on the pretense of helping Siranoush with last minute details. "That's an excellent idea, Turfanda," said Siranoush— the only thing missing was an exchange of winks. "Hazel...Kegham, why don't you two go out in the back yard and check the...," she was trying to say something relevant—"see if there's enough charcoal. Oh, yes, Hazel, here, take these bird seeds for the bird house. Clean the cushion on the swing. It's very relaxing. You might even see a few birds. Watch for a beautiful humming bird that shows up once in a while." Kegham's heart was pounding and to his surprise, no perspiration—a very good sign.

Mihran was dozing in the parlor. The *Detroit News* sport section was on his lap. The Detroit Tigers were playing the Cleveland Indians tomorrow at Navin Field.

Meanwhile, back at the Book Cadillac Hotel, the special East Coast guests were getting ready for dinner. Joan personally directed the florist as to how the bouquet of fresh-cut flowers was to be arranged. "Make sure it's delivered exactly at 5:45 p.m. at the Kevorkian residence, 119 Labelle Avenue. The attached card is to read, 'To our special and wonderful hosts, Siranoush and Mihran Kevorkian. George, Nellie, Joan, and Bob.' "

The florist looked at the floral arrangement, smiled, and thought, "Pretty good for an amateur."

George had never felt more like Kegham's father. His thoughts shifted to Rose. He envisioned a beaming, proud Rose relishing every time she was called "Mom."

Nellie lovingly watched George. She saw a kind and gentle husband. She even envisioned herself as a stepmother, but the thought lasted only for a fleeting moment.

Bob and George headed for the elevator. "See you ladies down in the lobby. We've got to be there at six p.m. sharp…my gastric juices are flooding my stomach!" Bob rubbed his stomach.

Both men headed for the two large chairs in the corner of the lobby and sank into down-filled cushions. Each, in his own way, felt pride and a sense of accomplishment that he had been a part of Kegham's life.

61

Dinner Diplomacy

It was a perfect day for barbequing—clear skies with wisps of balmy cool air; Indian summer is what the folks of the Midwest call it.

Rows of skewered lamb lay neatly on the grate. The orange glowing charcoal puffed steam and smoke as drops of oozing juice dripped on the hot coals.

Mihran shouted, "Siranoush, what time is it?"

"It's a little past 5:30." The plan was to have the kebabs ready by 6:15, allowing the guests time to get acquainted and be seated.

Siranoush noticed Hazel throwing glances from the kitchen window. "Hazel…." No response. "Hazel."

"Yes, Auntie?"

"Take the chefs some tea. Kegham likes one teaspoon of honey and Uncle Mihram likes his straight." Siranoush was using every opportunity to bring the two young people together.

Hazel stirred the honey in Kegham's cup with special care. "How sweet," mused Siranoush, as she turned all four burners off. The cast iron pots would keep their contents hot and ready for serving.

Six p.m.: The first to come were the Kuezians and Mardirosians. Just as Siranoush was greeting them, the taxi pulled up with the rest of the guest list. "Perfect timing," was Siranoush's greeting to her guests. Kegham was overflowing with joy and perspiration.

A dinner is a complete success when everyone is laughing and talking while eating and the host doesn't have to encourage second helpings. Guests just fill their plate and go on eating.

For some unknown reason, the usual exodus by the men to the parlor never happened. Instead, everyone remained seated while the table was cleared. For those who still had room in their digestive system, Siranoush brought in two plates of *kata*. "The coffee will be ready in a few minutes."

Bob was 100% convinced that Joan had a plan ready to unveil any minute. From the moment they arrived, Joan had been observing Hazel. She liked everything about her. She was exactly what Kegham needed. Joan knew in her heart that George, Rose, Bob, and herself had only been surrogates for the family Kegham had lost. This was his chance to fill that emptiness. Joan was not about to lose the opportunity to help make Kegham's hopes come true. Joan loved Kegham like a brother and tonight she was going to do her big-sister act. Nellie took the lead. "Mr. Mardirosian, you know that George is also in the shoe repair business."

199

Turfanda asked Nellie what kind of work she did. Nellie began explaining in English, but changed to Armenian. Hazel's parents had not fully mastered the English language, even though they had been in America since 1903.

Joan spoke to Nellie in limited, but understandable, Armenian that caught everyone by surprise – an *odar* (non-Armenian) speaking Armenian. This got everyone's attention. She started right into the mission's work; the guests sat listening spellbound to every word flowing from an energized Joan. Bob listened with pride as she described their work at the mission.

Kegham found temporary refuge by focusing on the plate of *kata* in front of him. Joan continued, "Bob and I have known Kegham for nearly 10 years. We love him just like a member of our family."

George added, "Kegham brought only joy and happiness to my sister Rose and me. We didn't know how empty our lives had been until that day he walked into our home. We became parents to Kegham and he lovingly called us Mom and Dad."

Joan and George conducted a running biography—the Silver Star, Purple Heart, his journey to America, etc. The only thing missing was a standing ovation.

Bob glowed with pride, "That's my Joan."

Harry made his trademark light-hearted comment, "I'm sorry to say, Kegham, you're ineligible to run for President of the United States."

Mihram immediately countered, "But he can run for Governor of Michigan." Hazel couldn't keep her eyes off of the perspiring, nervous wretch sitting across the table, whose stare was boring a hole right through the plate of *kata*.

Krikor's relaxed contented look sent Turfanda glowing with an inner joy.

Then Araxy continued, "Hazel, how old were you when you came to America?"

"Three years old, Auntie."

Araxy continued, "Hazel graduated from Troy High School."

"So did I!" shrieked Joan. "Remember Principal Jordan and his odd taste in ties, and Mrs. Eggleston. You know, she was completely bald and wore a wig."

"I didn't know that," answered Hazel. For a few minutes the two former graduates forgot the others whose heads were turning from one side of the table to the other trying to follow the rapid exchange of memories of Troy High.

Araxy wasn't through. "Do you know that Hazel was a volunteer Red Cross nurse during the war—and one of the first telephone operators on the Market Exchange in Detroit? Tell everyone about your present job, Hazel." Araxy held center stage. Hazel didn't have a chance. Araxy took another breath. "She's one of the top seamstresses at the exclusive Anderson Shop in the David Whitney Building—only the high-society ladies have their clothes made there. Tell them about Mrs. Henry Ford, Hazel." Araxy's enthusiasm was in overdrive. "Clara Ford's suits and dresses are sewn exclusively by Hazel." Hazel sat silently blushing on one side of the table while a perspiring Kegham sat on the other side of the table, his eyes still fixed on the plate of *kata*.

"Joan, you've met your match," chuckled Bob to himself. George, Nellie, and Bob were all convinced that Araxy and Joan were a perfect matchmaking team. The only thing missing now was the wedding date!

That night, Room 805 at the Book Cadillac Hotel was humming with happy talk. Everyone agreed that Hazel was right for Kegham. Krikor and Turfanda would be the kind of in-laws that Kegham could relate to. George added that Hazel's father was very impressed with Kegham's war record. When they finally finished evaluating the evening's events, Nellie put her arm around Joan. "Thank you, Joan, for leading the effort on Kegham's behalf."

George added, "Poor Kegham—did you see him perspiring and staring at the plate of *kata*?" Their laughter was only one full of love for the "groom."

Bob's face held a blank look. "I forgot why I came to Detroit—oh yes—the Herman Kiefer Hospital—something to do with medicine...I think." Laughter filled the room. It was the end of a perfect day.

62

Smooth Sailing

For the next eight months, the Agegian "Love Boat" sailed the tranquil seas of "first love." Then one glorious Saturday in June 1923, they were married at St. John's Episcopal Church with the full rites of the Armenian Apostolic Church. Father Levon made special arrangements to have a substitute priest hold services at St. Gregory's so he could officiate at Kegham's wedding.

The Armenian community of Detroit had not yet reached the numbers needed to have a church of their own. The Detroit Diocese of The Episcopal Church graciously let them hold services in their downtown cathedral on Sunday afternoons. It wouldn't be until 1932 that the newly built St. John the Baptist Armenian Apostolic Church would be consecrated.

Turfanda, Araxy, and Siranoush— matchmakers par excellence—wiped tears of joy as Hazel came down the aisle escorted by her proud father. George and Nellie were best man and matron of honor. George glowed with a father's pride standing next to his son, the "General." Rose was there by his side—there was no doubt of her presence.

Siranoush felt an odd mixture of melancholy and satisfaction as Mihran helped load their star boarder's few possessions into the car. The newlyweds would live with Hazel's parents for a while. They eventually found a lovely two-bedroom flat on Puritan Avenue, a short walk to Hazel's parents.

The landlord, Herman Amenz, was very accommodating to the newlyweds. He agreed to paint the rooms, install a new gas stove, and replace the old icebox with a brand new 50-pound box. There was more—the flat was completely furnished, with steam heat included, all for $60 a month. The two lovebirds chirped joyously as they moved into their "love nest."

Each morning the couple walked hand-in-hand the short distance to the Woodward Avenue streetcar line. Kegham got off at the Ford Motor plant at the Manchester Avenue stop. Hazel continued for another 20 minutes to Grand Circus Park, and a short walk to the David Whitney Building—up to the 14th floor and to the Anderson Shop. "Good morning, Hazel," was always the cheerful greeting from Mrs. Anderson—but this particular morning she paused for a closer look at her top seamstress. There was something different about her.

63

Happy and Sad Unfoldings

The sun's rays passed through the lace curtains, leaving geometric patterns on the bedroom floor. Hazel sat on the end of the bed as the doctor made his routine examination. "My guess is sometime in mid-June, next year, the Agegian's can expect the first addition to their family." Kegham was tingling all over. Hazel served a light lunch for Dr. Nalbandian. Family physicians were still making house calls in 1923.

The following month, Hazel gave her notice. "I'm going to be a full-time mother, Mrs. Anderson." "We're going to miss you, Hazel." Mrs. Anderson was more than an employer--the eight young ladies working there were like daughters. She later presented a new Singer sewing machine to Hazel to sew all her baby's clothes.

The months moved ever closer to that certain day in June 1924. Turfanda was a frequent visitor to her daughter's flat—helping and guiding her in the minutest ways. "Mother, I'm not an invalid. It's good for me to be active. The doctor said I should go on living a normal life," was Hazel's repeated plea.

"Nonsense!" was her mother's response. "Sit and relax while I do the washing," then quickly adding, "Just this time, I promise." A promise that somehow got lost between house cleaning, dinner preparations, dusting, and a few other household chores that were created by Turfanda's active mind to fill in her visits.

Hazel knew rebuking her mother's help would break her heart, so she sat on the sofa and "rested" as her mother had ordered. There were times the rest was a welcomed event. "Mothers know best."

Almost every Saturday was dinner at Hazel's parents' home. A warm and close relationship steadily grew between Turfanda and Kegham. In no time, he went from "*mer pessa*" (our son-in-law) to "*mer degha*" (our son).

Young Martin had taken to Kegham from the start. Kegham saw in Martin glimpses of his little brother, Setrak.

Letters to George and Nellie were full of kind words about his in-laws. George and Nellie laughed when one of the letters mentioned Turfanda's *kata* was almost as good as Rose's. George and Nellie couldn't be happier.

"I'm a pretty good judge of people—don't you think, Bob? I just knew Hazel was right for Kegham the minute I saw her." Bob looked at his wife, and sent one of his many signals of love. It felt so natural to be together.

One early morning, Araxy dropped in for a surprise visit. "How are our young mother and baby

doing?" Before Hazel could respond, she continued—
"I'm always available to help if you need any...."

Hazel interrupted, "You know my mom. She
has become my personal doctor, consultant, advisor,
and housekeeper."

"That's Turfanda," laughingly added Araxy.
"Hazel dear, may Martin go with Antranik to the
Barnum and Bailey Circus on Saturday?"

Hazel immediately responded, "That's great,
Araxy. But you'll have to go without me." She placed
both hands over her abdomen adding, "I don't think
I can come at this time."

"Don't worry, Hazel, I can handle the two
rascals." They laughed in agreement and continued
with their women talk.

The following Saturday morning, Martin
dashed up the stairs into his sister's open arms. Hazel
adored her little brother. She immediately began
combing his "Buster Brown" hair, adjusted his tie, and
made sure his knickers were of equal height over his
long stockings. Hazel stepped back for a better view.
"My little brother—the handsomest boy in Detroit."

Circus fever was pushing the joy meter to
maximum. Martin hugged and kissed his mother and
sister and bounded down the stairs behind Antranik.
Araxy added, "If it's all right, Turfanda, we're going
to have lunch at Sanders after the show."

Hazel hugged Araxy, "I'm tempted to go with you."

"Bye, Mama; bye, sister." The downstairs door closed abruptly, ending the voice of a jubilant Martin. The silence caught Hazel and her mother in a moment of unexpected contemplation. They stood staring down the long, empty staircase, each in her own private thoughts.

By Tuesday morning, Martin had developed a fever. Turfanda applied her old country remedy for colds: vinegar-soaked cloth wrapped around his feet and heavy layers of blankets to induce high body heat to break the fever.

By Wednesday morning, Martin was showing no signs of improvement. His life force was losing to a virulent infection. He was having difficulty breathing. "Mama—Mama..." his weakened voice tore Turfanda's heart to pieces.

Turfanda sat looking at the younger of her two remaining children. There were two others buried in a Troy, New York, cemetery; victims of illnesses that could not be medically helped at that time. Turfanda decided to go into perpetual mourning from that day on. She wore black for the rest of her life. In the evenings, the slow steady squeak of her rocker kept time to her voice as she sang the melancholy verses of long-forgotten songs, interrupted with sobs of deep longing, until her death in 1945.

Krikor was of a different temperament. "They're dead, woman. Let's get on with our lives," was his terse response to her spells of sadness. Sixteen years later, Krikor would be in his hospital bed with his wrists cuffed to the side rails, the only remedy for patients who kept pulling out oxygen tubes and IVs. He would grumble in silence, "Let this old man go and make room for someone else," and ending with his vast repertory of choicest expletives. He succumbed to the inevitable in his hospital bed in 1960.

Turfanda kissed Martin's forehead and rushed to Araxy's home. A panic-stricken, tearful Turfanda faced Araxy, "Martin is sick...Dr. Nalbandian...," she was trying to catch her breath. "Oh, God, hurry!"

Araxy immediately phoned Highland Park General Hospital. "Ambulance to 342 Buena Vista— hurry! It's an emergency!" Then a call to the doctor— "Dr. Nalbandian, this is Araxy Kuezian, very good friends of Krikor and Turfanda Mardirosian. Their son, Martin, is very ill—I called Highland Park General Hospital. The ambulance should be arriving any minute. Turfanda is here with me. We're going back to...."

Dr. Nalbandian cut into her frantic voice, "I'm leaving for the hospital immediately." In less than half an hour, Dr. Nalbandian was at Martin's bedside with Turfanda and Araxy. A quick examination and Martin was placed in the isolation ward—diagnosis: typhoid fever.

Hazel was preparing dinner when she began grimacing as labor pains gripped her abdomen. She decided to sit for a moment but ended lying on the bed. When the doorbell rang, she struggled to rise and slowly approached the speaker. "Yes?"

"It's Araxy, Hazel. Martin is at Highland Park General Hospital... I have a cab waiting... Hurry!"

Harry came home from work at 5:00 p.m. He read the hastily written note, "Get Kegham and Krikor and join Turfanda, Hazel, and me at Highland Park Hospital."

"You're wonderful, Harry," Araxy hugged her husband. "Without your note, I'd still be reading the sports section."

Dr. Nalbandian and two other doctors were talking in hushed voices in the hallway. Hazel's labor pains were becoming more frequent. Dr. Nalbandian went to the nurses' desk and within minutes, Hazel was lying in her own room attended by a nurse.

Thursday morning, June 26, Harry had left for work straight from the hospital, bleary-eyed and unshaven. Kegham had gotten permission from Mr. Bolton to be with Hazel until she gave birth. The ever-thoughtful Mr. Bolton added, "Take as long as necessary."

Araxy phoned Siranoush and asked if she would keep Antranik at her house until Saturday. "Don't worry; I'll take good care of him."

211

"Siranoush, I can't talk anymore—I'll explain later."

Siranoush immediately went to pick up Antranik. "What could it be?" She knew the baby was due soon. A very worried Siranoush walked Antranik back to her house. Straining to imagine what could be the problem that Araxy couldn't take a few minutes to explain set off a stream of speculations.

Friday evening, June 27, 1924, the unfolding of events was about to devastate the families with sadness at a time when only happiness and joy should have prevailed.

It was an easy birth. Hazel heard, for the first time, her baby's cries. "It's a healthy, handsome boy, my dear. My report will be 'Mother and baby are doing exceptionally well.'"

The assisting nurse cleaned the baby, and in minutes a tightly bundled newborn was whisked to the hospital nursery to join other new arrivals. Kegham was in tears. Hazel smiled at him, radiating a kind of affection that only the birth of a baby could bring forth.

Dr. Nalbandian quickly cleaned up and headed for the isolation ward and, as he passed the large observation window, he abruptly stopped and covered his face. Martin's bed was empty!

The crushing pall of sorrow pressed down mercilessly on Turfanda. Krikor cursed God, and wouldn't open his shoe repair store. Kegham had to open the store after work for a few days so that customers could claim their shoes. He left a note on the door: "Death in the Family."

Hazel was agonizing between the joys of her baby and the loss of her brother. Sometimes, during the week, the crushing weight of sadness would cause her to cry while nursing her baby. It was decided that her brother's name would live on in her own child.

With controlled emotions and unwavering dedication, Kegham became the beacon of light, helping the Mardirosian family to reach a safe harbor in a sea of sorrow.

In the years that followed, Martin became the focal point of four loving adults. He enjoyed playing cards, discussed politics, listened to stories of generals, kings and great events in history from his grandfather; from his grandmother who couldn't read but could recite by memory all of Jesus' parables while young Martin sat at her feet intently listening.

Victor Records brought to life Metropolitan Opera's great singers—Enrico Caruso, Geraldine Ferrar, Ernestine Schuman-Heick, John McCormack, Feodor Chaliapin and others. The music of Beethoven, Mozart, Offenbach, and Mendelssohn completed his home-schooling in classical music.

Martin would stand next to the Victrola with a firm grip on the crank, ready to turn it the second he detected the slightest change in the speed of the 78-rpm record. He only realized later in life how central he was to the happiness and hopes of his grandparents and parents. The bright light of his precious presence kept back the lurking shadows of past sorrows from his close-knit family.

64

Hit and Run

After lengthy discussions with Hazel, Kegham gave his notice to Ford Motor Company in 1928. Mr. Bolton wished Kegham well in his new venture, but silently wished he wouldn't leave.

They rented a small store under an apartment complex a few blocks from their flat and opened a dry-cleaning business. Hazel's skill as a seamstress easily handled repairs and alterations. Kegham taught himself how to press suits and dresses. With the help of a booming US economy, their business steadily grew.

They decided to move to a more spacious upstairs flat on 14th Street. At the same time, Hazel's parents moved to a small, tidy flat above an empty store at the busy intersection of Fenkell and Livernois Avenues. Krikor moved his shoe repair business into the store below. It turned out to be a wise move.

Each morning, Hazel would leave 4-year-old Martin in her mother's care, and head to the shop. Hazel learned to drive almost as easily as Kegham had done years ago in Watertown.

Kegham found what he unconsciously had been seeking all his life—a family of his own. The future abounded with hope and happiness—not to mention prosperity.

Then, on an October Friday in 1929, the stock market crashed. Its aftermath sent tremors throughout America. Savings accounts vanished behind closed bank doors. Factory output began its downward spiral. The increasing numbers of unemployed lined up in front of Ford, General Motors, and Chrysler plants. Life in America was heading for hard times.

In 1933, newly elected President Franklin D. Roosevelt took bold measures to revive the economy. His inaugural speech became the clarion call to his fellow citizens when he declared, "We have nothing to fear but fear itself." By 1934, unemployment was approaching 25% of the nation's work force.

Krikor's shoe repair and Kegham's dry-cleaning businesses eked out a living for both families through the early years of the "Great Depression." Mr. Lupo, a retired barber in the neighborhood, started giving haircuts from his parlor, at 50 cents for children and 75 cents for adults. Times were tough. The City of Detroit couldn't pay its employees in US currency and had to resort to scrip—printed facsimile of denominated money on typewriter paper. Butter cost 7 cents a quarter pound, milk was 10 cents a quart, bread was 6 cents a loaf, etc. Even at these prices, people had to buy on credit. The CCC, Civilian Conservation Corps, took many of the young unemployed off the streets to work in the national parks, highway repair, etc. The WPA, Works Project Administration, repaired city streets, sidewalks, and public buildings.

"Mom, I could give haircuts…just to the kids in the neighborhood…for only 25 cents." Hazel stopped cleaning the vegetables and looked at her son's earnest smiling face.

"What are you talking about, Martin?"

Martin's response was quick: "I can practice on Grandpa, and Dad, and…"

Hazel cut him short—"If you can get your dad to sit for a haircut…," she didn't finish. "Grandpa will let you do anything you want to him. You better start on him first."

The family gathered around Grandpa sitting near the potbelly stove in the dining room as Martin began clipping his first "victim."

In less than an hour, an elegant grandfather, with trimmed mustache thrown in for good measure, was smiling approvingly as he checked every inch of his head in the mirror held by his proud grandson.

Turfanda peeked in from the kitchen. "My darling can do anything. Clean up! Dinner is almost ready."

Martin learned to shine shoes at Grandpa's store. He had an excellent teacher—Albert, a tall, lanky, elderly African American who would make all sorts of snapping sounds with the polishing cloth and clicking sounds from the two brushes that skimmed over, around, and behind the shoes in unbroken rhythmic movements.

"Albert, I got a tip!"

"Yo sho loin fass, boy. Sho glad yo is woiking only on Satadays." Albert gave Martin a pat on the back and continued blocking and cleaning men's felt hats, which was his area of expertise.

Finally Kegham reluctantly volunteered and ended up surprisingly satisfied with his haircut. Nersess, the neighbor downstairs, was a photo engraver and made an official-looking diploma that read, "14th Street Barber College." Mom and Dad signed their official approvals in the spaces provided. Grandpa got a used hand clipper. Mom supplied a small scissor and comb. Dad contributed a new, wide-bristled paint brush to whisk away hair clippings, and Grandma donated a bed sheet. Martin was in business.

Word got around of another barber on 14th Street. The sign read "Haircuts for Kids only – 25 cents." The location of the barber shop was truly unique. The young customers, clutching their coins, sat on an orange crate in the basement next to the furnace under a single light bulb hanging from the ceiling. Martin also rented his comic books at a penny a day. In no time, a steady stream of customers developed. Mothers still could recognize their children after coming home from Martin's Basement Barber Shop.

Pennies, nickels, dimes, and quarters were counted and deposited in a tin cigar box under his socks in his dresser drawer. Kegham would watch from the hallway as Martin would calculate—two dollars times 52 weeks, 104—3 x 52—4 x 52. Past memories brought a smile to Kegham's face. "It won't be long before 14th Street has its first millionaire."

By the end of 1932, 14th Street had slowly become a disaster zone. Repossessed automobiles, minus the distributor caps, rested on cement blocks, slowly turning into useless hulks of rusted metal and rotted wood. The bank made sure that no one could drive unless payments were forthcoming.

One bright bit of news was the promised "Soldier's Bonus." The much anticipated day found the war veterans eagerly waiting for the postman and the $200 US Treasury check.

The fathers of the German families watched as their neighbors rejoiced—they had the misfortune to have served on the wrong side. In less than eight years, their sons would be fighting for America against the Fatherland.

It was a typical evening. Kegham dropped Hazel and Martin off at Grandma's. After parking the car, he headed toward Grandma's house. The light turned red. He started to cross the street. The last thing he heard and saw was the ominous sound of screeching tires and the sudden blaze of headlights.

Hazel kept looking out of the window to the street below, anxiously waiting for signs of Kegham. "Mama, what's keeping him—it's been almost half an hour."

Turfanda stirred the pot, "Don't worry, he's on his way."

Downstairs, one of Krikor's customers dropped in to report a hit-and-run accident a few blocks away. "The poor fellow's body was thrown 40 feet against the opposite curb."

Krikor's comment was, "Another drunk driver," and continued ripping off worn rubber heels.

Kegham's driver's license led the police to the 14th Street address. The Nersessians downstairs directed them to Hazel's parents' flat. "They're there every Saturday night," said a distraught Arshalous.

The police car raced towards Livernois and Fenkell Avenues. The officers did their best to calm an hysterical wife and frightened son as they headed for the Redford Township Receiving Hospital.

Mother and son spent the next seven hours steeped in anxiety. Finally, they were led into a nearly empty ward. At one end was a sight that 10-year-old Martin would never forget.

His father lay propped up in a fresh body cast with openings only for his eyes, nose, and mouth. Hazel gasped for air.

Without any greeting or introduction, the attending doctor started, "I don't see how your husband survived the accident—let alone having reached the hospital alive." His cold, impersonal analysis faded into the ether. Hazel could only silently cry out her sounds of sorrow and emotional pain while a tearful, frightened son looked on.

Next followed the doctor's grim diagnosis without the slightest tinge of compassion in his voice. "Four dislocated vertebra—several compound fractures of the right leg, with splintered tibia— possible amputation. Right arm and shoulder compound fractures...," he paused to read a comment. "Previous injury indicated on shoulder blade—incision front and back on left side." He took a breath and continued, "Multiple concussions to the head—three broken and six cracked ribs and a severely dislocated right hip."

The doctor removed his glasses and turned to his colleague. "It's a miracle this man made it through the operations alive." His colleague gave a quick look at the plaster "mummy" and shook his head in agreement.

Martin clung to his mother's arm while his father clung to life inside his plaster prison. The ward was nearly empty except for a few patients at the far end, whose eyes focused intently on the unfolding drama past the rows of empty beds. Invisible streams of sympathy flowed towards the white curtains surrounding Kegham's bed. A thoughtful nurse made beds available for mother and son next to Kegham. It was 8 o'clock Sunday morning.

Hazel had gained her composure long enough to phone the Nersessians. "Arshalous!"

"Hazel, what is it?! Why are you crying?"

"Arshalous, please let my parents know that Martin and I are staying at the hospital. They've been very kind…" her sobs wouldn't let her continue.

Arshalous interrupted, "What hospital?"

"Oh, Arshalous, Kegham was hit by a car…"

"What can we do to help? Anything, please, Hazel…." Rampaging emotions prevented Hazel to continue.

A young doctor approached a weary Hazel. Her tired distraught face looked up silently pleading for answers. "Mrs. Agegian, I'm Dr. Morrison. I've been assigned your husband's case. I'm going to do everything possible to help your husband back to health."

Before Hazel could respond, the moment was suddenly charged with excitement. It was Kegham's voice! He spoke slowly, in Armenian, "Don't let them cut my leg off." He had been just conscious enough to hear the word "amputation."

"What did your husband say?" interjected Dr. Morrison, who was elated and amazed that his patient was conscious, let alone speaking.

Kegham's faint rasping voice continued in English, "I'll never find a job."

A broad smile covered Dr. Morrison's face. He put his arm around Hazel. "Mrs. Agegian, your husband has already started on the road to recovery. Anyone who can think that far ahead in the condition he's in is a real survivor." Hazel devoured every word coming from the young doctor. It was what she desperately needed to hear.

In the ensuing 14 months, Kegham gradually shed his cast. Dr. Morrison fought the threat of gangrene several times and at one time he even contemplated amputation. The multiple problems facing patient and doctor soon gave way to Dr. Morrison's professional skills and an unwavering dedication to his patient's welfare.

It was decided that any news of Kegham's situation go no farther than Detroit's City limits. George and Nellie, Bob and Joan were to be kept lovingly in the dark—for the present.

Every Saturday and Sunday, mother and son would make the one-and-a-half-hour, one-way street car ride, with two transfers, to reach the hospital. "Mrs. Agegian, you can't imagine the importance of your visits. There is no lab test that can measure their therapeutic effects." Dr. Morrison's confident voice was so reassuring both in word and tone. Just to see Dr. Morrison would be enough to give Hazel a much needed boost to carry on with renewed energy.

"Honey, I think I'll close my eyes for a while." Hazel reached for her husband's hand. Kegham watched through seemingly closed eyes and slipped down memory lane. He saw himself glued to the stairs and looking up into Hazel's smiling face. "Hello, Kegham, I'm glad you were able to come." The thin sliver of light faded as sleep overcame a tired, weary, pain-ridden body.

The economic depression continued, strangling the hopes and vitality of millions of American families. The burden of survival fell mercilessly on Hazel's shoulders. Their dry cleaning business was sold at a fraction of their initial investment. It was a paltry sum, but "cash was king." Without asking, their landlord cut the rent from $35 to $8 and then to $5 a month. The bank was going to foreclose anyway.

After several missed payments, Detroit Edison turned off the electricity. Candles became the only source of light in many of the homes on 14th Street. Hazel kept their gas and water meter turning—she had no intention of burdening her husband with such "trivial" matters, as she reminded herself every chance she got. During their first winter, mother and son retreated to the kitchen. Martin slept under the legs of the gas stove on a mattress of several blankets and Hazel on a folding canvas cot. On cold nights, the heat from the open oven door kept the small kitchen heated. An apple crate nailed to the outside window sill was their ice box—just open the window and reach in—how convenient!

The Singer shortened, lengthened, and repaired. The quality of Hazel's work guaranteed a small but adequate income. "Thanks, Mrs. Anderson." Martin's basement barber shop continued to fill the cigar box with coins.

Then there was always tenacious Turfanda who rode the Fenkell streetcar line as far as 14th Street and then walked six blocks to her daughter's flat with hot food. Always unannounced but always welcomed.

Shopping with Grandma was an adventure. Her technique was simple—ignore the disgruntled, angry clerks and go for the freshest or "no sale." Anything that could be squeezed, sniffed, thumped, or tasted was put to the test. Milk bottle caps were unceremoniously opened until one was found without "caked" cream inside the lid. Caked cream meant at least three-day-old milk. "See, Martin, my sweet—here's a clear cap—we'll take this one." The frustrated clerk's admonition fell on deaf ears. Grandma moved on to assault the innocent vegetables and hapless fruit which would feel the full force of the squeeze, thump, and sniff test.

It was different at Gus Schaeffer's butcher store. As soon as Mr. Schaeffer spotted Turfanda crossing the street, he knew exactly which chicken to pull out of the cage. "A beauty, Mrs. Mardirosian."

Mr. Schaeffer held the struggling Plymouth Rock hen as she squeezed the breasts and thighs—a short pause—"Good." In a split second, a headless chicken, its legs tied, was hanging from a hook inside the rim of a large steel drum, whirling, spinning and thumping its life away.

Next, it was plunged into a huge pot of boiling water for a few minutes, and then plucked clean. The heart, liver, and gizzard, cleaned of gravel, were tossed inside the hollow gutted chicken. It all took less than 10 minutes from "good" to "goodbye, Mr. Schaeffer."

Fish also came live. In a large tank, fish lazily swam while the customers peered down, deciding which one was to be that night's dinner. Turfanda only needed to point at the fish in question—the attendant scooped up the fish in a cup-shaped net. From tank to frying pan, an absolutely fresh fish without hook, bait, or rented row boat. This was shopping for dinner in America before mass production, freezers, dated plastic wrap, and ladies like Turfanda, who had made shopping a precise art.

65

From Cast to Crutch to Cane

Nersess' Model A Ford headed for Redford Receiving Hospital. Hazel sat silent, wrapped up in her thoughts. Kegham was finally coming home.

"He did it, Mrs. Agegian."

"No, Doctor Morrison. The credit goes to you, and no one else," was Hazel's grateful response.

The back seat was lined with pillows to accommodate Kegham's trip home. Nersess said, "Arshalous is ready to help anytime—whether you want it or not." He laughed, as did Hazel between sobs. Nersess turned to Hazel, "Just get Kegham strong and walking again. There's a lot of hard work still ahead. Arshalous always said she wanted to be a nurse. Now she has her chance," laughingly adding, "and with on-the-job training." His words radiated confidence. Hazel felt a sense of relief come over her, bolstering her resolve to face the difficult days ahead.

The home front was in good shape. The electric meter was turning along with the gas and water meters. Life had moved from the kitchen to the rest of the house. The family was together under one roof— nothing else mattered.

"Hazel, stand right here and don't move." Kegham leaned on his crutches; a serious look was trying to cover a moment of joy that was soon to erupt.

Kegham's military tone of voice continued,
"Private…I mean…Sergeant Hazel Agegian, please
stand at attention—this is serious business."

Hazel couldn't resist laughing, "What's this all
about?" "You are not to interrupt," ordered Kegham.

"Corporal!" In strutted Martin, holding a small
black rectangular box. "Reporting as ordered,
General." Martin was struggling to stop the pressing
need to shout.

"Now, wipe that silly smile off your face."

"Yes, sir, General." Martin snapped to
attention, and held out the black box holding his
father's Silver Star. Hazel started to cry—she saw
what was coming. Tears began filling Kegham's
eyes—Martin hugged his mom.

Kegham cleared his throat. "For bravely
carrying out your duties, against impossible odds, and
bringing so much happiness to our family—you are
hereby awarded the Silver Star" and quickly pinned it
on Hazel's dress. Joyous tears flowed freely.
Happiness born of sacrifice and love heals heartaches,
strengthens resolve, and triumphs over tragedy—
economic depression, physical handicap, and an
uncertain future all dissolved the moment Kegham
wrapped his arms around his wife and son.

In the months that followed, Kegham shed his
leg cast and exchanged his crutches for a cane. He
walked all the way to the Ford plant. Mr. Bolton had

retired some time ago. The Employee Relations Program was non-existent. The cruel reality was that a man leaning on a cane was out of place in the unemployment line. Frustration slowly gave way to depression. Not being able to contribute to his family's welfare was the reality most difficult to face.

George and Nellie were still unaware of Kegham's injury. George's letter ended, "We miss you, son. All our love to Hazel and Martin. PS, one of my customers mentioned an opening for night watchman's job—300 applicants lined up the day it was posted. How's your business doing? I'm still ripping off soles and heels. Nellie is working full time at the law firm." Bob and Joan were equally kept in the dark about the accident and its debilitating aftermath.

One day as Kegham sat watching Hazel at the sewing machine, her hand adeptly moved the torn trouser back and forth until the hole was meticulously repaired. For some unknown reason the words of Dr. Morrison came to mind, "Anyone who can think that far ahead in his condition is a real survivor."

The survival word had a stimulating effect on Kegham. The slow slide into depression was halted. Joan's words crowded his thoughts. It was like a mental life preserver. "You have proven your ability to overcome tragedy and sadness the likes of which few people experience. You were strong as a boy and now even stronger as a man—don't let your drive to survive weaken."

Kegham leaped out of his chair and limped towards Hazel. He smiled at a startled Hazel and pressed her hand. Hazel was trying to understand the sudden change in her husband. "Hazel—I'm going to go back to Watertown to look for a job."

Hazel's face froze in full panic mode. Kegham continued, "I'm sure I can find a job. I'll stay with George and Nellie."

Hazel's immediate response was, "We can't afford the train fare."

Kegham calmly replied, "I'll hop the freight cars like other unemployed men are doing. It's very simple."

Hazel's eyes bulged with tears. Kegham held her face in his hands, "Please understand, I can't quit…never!" Never was said with such finality that all that was left was to start packing his suitcase.

The next day, Kegham bid his family good-bye and headed for the Michigan Central rail yards. He had $10 in his pocket and a shoe box of sandwiches prepared by Turfanda, who thought he was crazy to go.

Almost 18 years later and here he was with $10 in his pocket and a box full of food again leaving behind loved ones on a journey fraught with unknowns.

This time it wasn't an Argentinean freighter but an American boxcar, and all you needed to know was if it was heading east. Helping hands from fellow veterans were ready to pull him aboard. Railroad company police more often than not turned a blind eye at the desperate men and even directed them to the cars going to specific cities. Fellow veterans weren't about to forsake their wartime comrades.

Postal money orders began arriving regularly. Nellie's boss found Kegham several part time jobs— George, with the help of one of his customers, provided leads for more work. "Hazel, I'm able to walk longer periods without my cane," wrote Kegham. Hazel finished reading and pressed the letter to her breast and continued sewing.

A Christmas card arrived from Danville, Vermont. Hazel's heart did cartwheels. It wasn't the $100 postal money order, or the warm greetings from Bob and Joan...it was Kegham's closing words, "I'll be home soon. I miss my family so very much. I'm sure I can find work in Detroit. No boxcars this time...it's Pullman coach all the way. Hugs and Kisses, Kegham. God Bless Amerika!"

66

Could It Be Possible?

Kegham leaned on his cane and, with his other hand, grasped the leather strap holding the suitcase together. A slight shiver skipped through him as he stepped out of the train station into Detroit's cold January air. "15790 14th Street, driver." The taxi turned north on Woodward Avenue. At Manchester Avenue, the light changed to red. Kegham had a few moments to observe the long line of men in front of the same gate he used to drive out to work every morning 12 years earlier.

The cabbie interrupted his thoughts, "It's like that Monday thru Friday. Some even sleep overnight so as not to lose their place in line."

The light changed. Kegham settled back, happily anticipating being home again. He hadn't seen his family for over six months.

As the cab turned down 14th Street, Kegham spotted Martin building a snowman. "Stop! Stop!" The cab slid over the snow-lined street and came to an abrupt stop. Kegham apologized, "I'm sorry, driver. My plans were to surprise my family. I see my son has already seen me"—and quickly paid the fare.

"Dad! Dad!" Martin ran pell-mell into his father's outstretched arms. The impact sent father and son falling into a snow drift. They lay in the snow laughing. The moment embodied a love between father and son that never diminished.

Mr. Gardner, the old Civil War veteran, smiled as he watched father and son from his living room window. Every 4th of July, the neighborhood children would gather in front of his house, exactly at noon, hoping to be one of the few who would be selected to wear parts of Mr. Gardner's Union Army uniform—a cap, coat, jacket, belt, etc. Mr. Gardener would strap on his leather belt with the attached scabbard and sword. A cluster of neighbors would gather to watch the flag-raising ceremony. Women and children placed their hands over their hearts, and war veterans stood erect, holding their salute until the flag reached the top of the pole.

Henry Jacob Gardner died a few years later, and with his passing, so did the special 4th of July commemoration on 14th Street.

Martin proudly carried his father's suitcase as they trudged through the snow-covered sidewalk. "Remember what I told you to do." A mischievous glow covered Martin's face as he waited until his father disappeared around the side of the house.

Two stairs at a time and Martin was up in his room. He grabbed the clear glass ball filled with water which, when shaken, released little white flakes resembling snow on a miniature log cabin inside.

Hazel came in from the kitchen to where Martin was sitting. "Did you finish making your snowman already?"

"Mom! Look what I see." He was intently concentrating on the glass ball. Hazel smiled and started to turn back towards the kitchen. "Mom! Mom! You won't believe what I'm seeing!"
A moment of curiosity turned Hazel back towards the living room.

"What do you see?"

Martin screamed, "It's Dad, and I can see him through the log cabin's window."

Hazel didn't know how to react to a lonely boy hallucinating about seeing his father. Her own moment of loneliness caught her off guard.

Sounds from the kitchen. Hazel turned. Kegham's voice pierced the air, "How long does a hungry traveler have to wait before being served dinner in this four-star hotel?"

Hazel's legs weakened. She barely reached the sofa. Martin shouted, "Surprise!"

Hazel sat paralyzed, unable to move or speak.

For the next hour, the foundation of 15790 - 14th Street rocked—the Nersessians came upstairs to welcome Kegham home.

That night, the sleep meter needle was stuck on "wide-awake." At 3:00 a.m., it was all over—the needle was heading for "deep sleep." Kegham's last thoughts were, "I need to find a framed 'Home Sweet Home' tomorrow."

It was becoming begrudgingly clear that jobs in Detroit were still not for a man hobbling on a cane. Kegham's self-esteem was being battered and its effects were beginning to show on his face.

One day, waiting for the streetcar after a long disappointing day looking for employment, Kegham noticed a sign being placed in the window of an all-night diner across the street—"Wanted-Dishwasher."

The unshaven, gruff-sounding cook bellowed out, "It's only for one month, 6 p.m. to 6 a.m. Monday through Friday. Eight dollars a day and all you can eat. Oh yeah, sweep and mop the floor before leaving."

His life was being reduced to that of a cripple begging for work. His physical handicap was challenging enough, but it was the insidious feeling of guilt that was driving Kegham deeper into desperation that hurt the most. Hazel vowed never to let her actions or words add to her husband's hardships.

The frost had etched its geometric patterns on the corners of the windows. Eleven a.m. and Kegham was still in bed. Usually, he'd be up, dressed and out by eight a.m. "Kegham, don't you think it's too cold to go out today?" No response. She continued sewing. Then, the words she wanted to hear.

"You're right, Hazel. I think I'll go to the library today." A relieved Hazel pedaled her Singer sewing machine as the needle moved at lightning speed across a knee patch on a child's torn trousers.

Kegham finished his breakfast, and hugged Hazel. "I'll be home in a few hours."

The steady cadence of one step at a time down the long staircase ended with the sound of the front door closing. The silence brought on a feeling of sadness that was difficult for Hazel to bear.

The Francis Parkman branch library was a haven for many of the unemployed men—an escape from the uncertainties facing their daily lives. It offered a warm, peaceful atmosphere to relax and read. The long walk over icy sidewalks to the library drained Kegham's stamina. He headed for the nearest table, removed his army coat, and hung his cane on the back of the chair for a moment of rest before going to the magazine section and the latest *National Geographic.* The morning edition of *The Detroit Free Press* was on the table. Kegham scanned the pages. Unemployment in Detroit was passing the national average of 25%, causing growing worker unrest. Earl Browder, chairman of the American Communist Party, was spreading the party line—anti-capitalism, anti-American and pro-Soviet Union propaganda. The United Automobile Workers (UAW) was gathering strength under the leadership of its first president, Walter Reuther.

The Big Three auto companies refused to recognize any form of unionism. Strike breakers were hired, spreading havoc and violence against the picketing workers. Kegham reached the last page and leaned back in his chair. Time to head to the magazine section.

As he rose, his eyes focused on a short article. He stopped and settled back into the chair. The first sentence began with "Robert Columbo has been appointed Vice President in charge of the legal division of the Ford Motor Company, Dearborn, Michigan....a graduate of Harvard Law School...." He reread the article—then, the name—Robert—no, Bob—no, Brother Bob! The present disappeared. The past pulled him back 17 years—the Western Front— Company D. The jumble of images crowded into his mind. His pulse began pounding. Could it be possible???

Kegham's gaze was transfixed on the librarian. She happened to look up and began wondering why she was the object of such intense scrutiny.

Kegham rose and limped towards her desk. "Excuse me, ma'am. May I have a sheet of blank paper?" and then hesitatingly added, "an envelope and a pencil—please?"

Her response belied the kind and helpful demeanor of librarians everywhere. From her desk drawer, she pulled out several sheets of paper, an envelope and a needle-sharp No. 2 pencil and laid them in front of Kegham. She spoke in a librarian's gentle, hushed voice, "If there's anything else you need, young man, please don't hesitate to ask."

She looked old enough to be his mother. He wanted to hug her. For the next hour, Kegham was totally engrossed in writing. Then came a moment of panic—maybe this Robert Columbo was not Brother Bob! Finally, he finished. He reread it several times, sealed the envelope and addressed it to: Mr. Robert Columbo, Vice President Legal Department—Ford Motor Company, Dearborn, Michigan.

An inner joy of anticipation was beginning to build. "Thank you very much, Miss Finlay." Her name was prominently displayed on her desk.

"You're welcome, and if you wish, I can add your letter to the library's outgoing mail tonight." It was an unexpected moment of embarrassment; Kegham didn't have a cent on him to pay for the stamp, but he bravely reached into his pocket.

Miss Finlay was a step ahead. Her instinct was in full control. Her soft voice continued, "It's alright, I'm sure the library can afford one three-cent stamp." Miss Finlay carefully placed the stamp on the envelope and dropped it in the "outgoing mail" box. She looked up as they both exchanged smiles.

"Thank you, Miss Finlay."

Miss Finlay had noticed to whom the letter was addressed. She pressed her thumb on the Lincoln three-cent stamp to make sure it was firmly attached, and silently wished success to its contents.

The cold air and the long walk home hardly mattered. Glimmers of hope were beginning to surface. Kegham's limp seemed to vanish as he walked over the icy, snow-covered sidewalks all the way home, singing the field artillery song. True to his secretive nature, he didn't say a word to Hazel about the letter. He enjoyed secrets. His thoughts were of Brother Bob the rest of the night. As soon as Hazel was asleep, he looked up at the ceiling. All he saw was a man sitting behind a large desk signing papers— he looked like someone he knew, but he wasn't sure who he was. He struggled to recognize the person behind the desk for some time until sleep overcame him.

67

Yes, It's Possible

At Hally Elementary School, every pair of eyes in Miss Short's 5th-grade arithmetic class watched the wall clock next to George Washington's portrait. The minute hand moved one minute at a time…click—2:57…click—2:58…click—2:59…one more click and the shrill final bell would resonate throughout the two-story building declaring the moment of liberation for children and teachers alike.

For Martin, it was full speed for home, up the front stairs, a quick "Hi, Mom," then to his room, off with school clothes, on with play clothes, then scampering down the back stairs through Arshalous' kitchen, and plunk down on a pillow in front of the Atwater Kent radio speaker. Also waiting was a tray with a glass of Ovaltine and a plate of ginger snap cookies. What more could a 10-year-old boy ask for? For the next two hours, the radio dial moved between WJR, WWJ, and WXYZ for the day's episodes of Jack Armstrong, the All-American Boy, The Adventures of Little Orphan Annie, Chandu the Magician, Buck Rodgers in the 25th Century, King of the Royal Mounties, The Lone Ranger...etc. The power of concentration and creative imagination was all a young listener needed to bring to life: fistfights, gun battles, and moments of suspense, mysterious sounds, galloping horses, rain, thunder, wind, explosions, footsteps over gravel, wooden floors and grass,

240

creaking chairs, and doors. Then, at the climactic moment, when Tarzan had just fallen into a deep pit filled with poisonous snakes, or Buck Rodgers' space ship was seconds away from disintegrating, the background music swelled to a crescendo and young Americans across four time-zones held their breath and listened to a clear articulate voice as it calmly announced, "Will the Lone Ranger be able to save Tonto's life from the burning barn?" There was a short pause—"Listen tomorrow, boys and girls, for the next exciting episode of 'The Lone Ranger.' 'Hi-Oh Silver, Awaaay.'" Rossini's *William Tell Overture* ended the episode. Intermission and time for some Ovaltine and crunchy ginger snap cookies. Arshalous enjoyed watching Martin and silently wished that she'd have a son just like him someday.

Hazel peeked from the kitchen at Kegham sitting on the living room sofa, visibly absorbed in deep contemplation. She figured his behavior had changed the day after he came back from the library, but she wasn't quite sure. It was puzzling her and she was determined to find the reason.

For Kegham, the moments of contemplation were a result of a growing doubt that it was just coincidence. He envisioned the Vice President's secretary dropping his letter into the waste paper basket—the final destination for all irrelevant mail.

He began calculating—Miss Finlay mailed his letter Friday night. "Let's see—Saturday, Sunday, Monday—possibly Tuesday...I should hear from

Brother Bob…" Then an over-powering fear gripped him—"Did I forget to write my address on the envelope? No! No! No!" With a great effort, he convinced himself that he hadn't forgotten. Anyway, kind, alert Miss Finlay would have noticed it and brought it to his attention. Kegham continued with his calculations, "I should know by Wednesday or no later than Thursday."

It all made sense. He laid his head back against the sofa, closed his eyes and saw Brother Bob sitting behind a big desk reaching out to shake his hand. "No. No. No—let's try that again." This time it was a smiling Brother Bob racing out of his office hugging him—"Yes, that's more like it!"

Wednesday morning—Martin had already left for school. Kegham was shaving and Hazel had started to pin the tissue dress pattern on one of her customer's dress material. The doorbell buzzer startled Hazel. "Yes?"

"I'm here to drive Mr. Agegian to Mr. Columbo's office."

"Did you say Mr. Columbo?" Kegham rushed from the bathroom. Hazel stepped aside, totally confused.

A smiling young man looked up at Kegham standing at the head of the stairs, with razor in hand and soap-covered face.

An ecstatic Kegham turned to Hazel, "Its Brother Bob! I'll explain later." In minutes, Kegham was bounding down the stairs.

The door slammed shut with a loud bang. The silence this time was to be the prelude to important and wonderful news. Hazel hummed to herself as she cut around the sleeve pattern of a dress. Then a most pleasant shock, "Kegham, you forgot your cane!"

The driver's eyes kept shifting between the road and the rearview mirror as he pushed his deductive powers to its limits, wondering "What is the connection between this nondescript foreigner (Kegham never lost his accent) living in an upstairs flat and Mr. Columbo?"

He waited for his passenger to start a conversation, but Kegham was somewhere between planet Earth and outer space. All he could think of was, "Vice President Robert Columbo—Vice President Bob—Brother Bob, Vice President." His heart was pounding. There was a steady flow of perspiration and no handkerchief—"God, I forgot my cane!"

The Lincoln silently sped down US Highway 12 towards Ford's Dearborn plant. A few more miles of silence. The driver kept shifting his eyes between the road ahead and the rear-view mirror.

Finally, he broke the silence. "I'm Arnold Johnson. I'm doing my law school internship in

Mr. Columbo's office. I graduated from the
University of Michigan last June." Kegham sent
a smile into the rearview mirror. "Sir, did I pronounce
your name correctly? It's Armenian, isn't it—almost
all Armenian names end in 'ian.' I had two classmates
in high school—Andy Topalian and Armen
Barsamian."

It was quite clear to Kegham that the young
intern wanted to know his relationship to the Vice
President. So, Kegham finally decided to help the
struggling Sherlock Holmes. "Mr. Johnson, did you
know that Mr. Columbo was awarded the Purple Heart
during the war by General Pershing himself? We
served in the same unit together." The Lincoln was
halfway into the next lane, but swerved back again.

"Wow," exclaimed young Arnold. Kegham's
expression sent a friendly message, "Keep your eyes
on the road, young man."

They passed the guard at the gate and in
seconds the Lincoln pulled into a space marked
"Reserved—Robert Columbo."

"Mr. Columbo will be with you in about an
hour. He's at a meeting. I thought you'd like to have
some breakfast in the executive cafeteria—we still
have time."

They found a table and sat down. A waiter
came to take their order. The next scene was right out
of the past—the cafeteria doors flew open—Brother

Bob came running but this time, not in a wheelchair, "You son-of-a-gun," and they hugged, laughed, and hugged again. "Thanks for taking good care of my Brother Kegham, Arnold."

"Yes, sir, my pleasure." The brothers disappeared into the vice president's office.

They sat looking at each other trying to remember the past. Kegham's letter had explained everything, but Bob insisted on knowing the details. In the next two hours Kegham told the story of his life—every time he'd say, "That's not important," Bob insisted that he continue.

"Don't stop. I want to know everything. After hearing how you came across my name, I'm convinced that our lives are directed by a higher force. Everything is connected." Bob moved his chair closer to Kegham. "I haven't been idle. I've found you a position that's perfect for you." Kegham was filled with pride, respect, and an inner joy that was radiating throughout his body. "Starting next week, you'll be the foreman of the Upholstery Department—you'll have your own office, and..." Kegham was shaking with pent-up emotion.

Bob was caught off guard. "Kegham, you know how emotional we Italians are. If Mr. Ford should come in and see us both crying over the plush carpet he was nice enough to put in my office—I'll be fired and you'll never be foreman of the Upholstery Department."

Time raced back to 1918. They began reliving their army experiences. It was a source of great, joyful nostalgia. They hadn't realized how close a relationship the five brothers had developed until they recalled all the events that had bonded them together. Bob mused, "I sure miss them." There was a moment of silence.

Bob checked his watch. "Kegham, your family must be wondering what happened to you." As if foreman of the Upholstery Department wasn't enough, Bob continued, "Here's your schedule for the next 30 days. Arnold will pick you up every morning at 7:00 a.m." Kegham was about to react, but Bob quickly cut him off—"Soldier, I don't want a peep out of you. You're to follow orders and no questions— understand?" He leaned over to Kegham, "Please don't say another word—I can't do enough for the brother who risked his life for me."

Bob continued, "Every Friday, you will receive physical therapy. The doctor assured me you'll be able to drive a car, which I've arranged for you— sorry, but I couldn't manage a chauffeur." Kegham was speechless. Bob's smiling face shown like a beacon as they embraced, and young Arnold cheerfully added, "See you Monday at 7 a.m., Mr. Agegian."

"I'll be ready, Mr. Johnson."

A steady vigil was being kept back home. Mother and son had been glued to the living room window. The excitement meter had already broken its

246

spring and now the anxiety-meter needle was pushing against the stop in the red zone.

"Mom! Mom!" Hazel rushed from the kitchen to the living room window. Kegham was just getting out of the car. In seconds, his family was hugging him down on the front porch.

Hazel's excited voice could barely form words. "Tell me about Mr. Columbo." The family clung to each other all the way up the narrow staircase.

Kegham dropped exhausted on the sofa. "Hazel, there's so much to tell you; so much has happened. It's unbelievable. Last Friday, remember how cold it was?" Every detail was meticulously recounted. Then the electrifying words—Foreman of the Upholstery Department—Hazel broke down; Martin cheered. Kegham remembered Bob slipping an envelope into his coat pocket when they had parted. The short note read, "Brother Kegham, take your family out for dinner. I'll see you Monday." They all stared at the crisp one hundred dollar bill that accompanied the note. Ol' Ben Franklin seemed to be smiling back!

"Okay! Are we ready to go out and celebrate?" Kegham's voice quivered with every word. The future of the Agegian family had suddenly and dramatically changed.

68

Changes in the Wind

The following year brought unimaginable economic stability for the family. Kegham proved his ability to run the upholstery department from the very first week. Bob glowed with pride with every favorable report. Blood brothers couldn't be any closer.

Kegham familiarized himself with the workers' rights under the union contract and on occasion substituted his own interpretation in situations not covered under the terms of the contract. The workers never forgot those occasions of fairness and understanding. Somehow along the way, Kegham became "Dick" to his co-workers. It didn't matter—he was still Kegham to his family and friends.

1938--Europe was precariously tilting towards war. The German chancellor, Adolph Hitler, used his evil genius, coupled with shrewd political daring, to cast aside the restrictions placed on Germany, after her defeat, in 1918, against military expansion beyond 100,000 troops. In a series of bold moves, he regained lost territories and absorbed two sovereign nations, Czechoslovakia and Austria, without firing a shot. Hitler's iron will became a power to be reckoned with in Europe. The beginning words in the German National Anthem, *"Deutschland uber Alles"* (Germany Above All) became the conscious embodiment at all levels of German society, and, if that wasn't enough, cast on each soldier's metal belt buckle were the words, "Gott mitt uns" (God with us), a constant reminder whose side the Almighty favored.

There were no hidden agendas. It was "Europe today—tomorrow the world." Hitler boasted a thousand years of German hegemony in Europe. His boast only lasted 12 years, ending with the defeat and near total destruction of the German "Fatherland."

Kegham received a short note from Bob, "Meet me at Luke's Diner after work." Bob's car was already in the parking lot when Kegham pulled in. Bob waved from a corner booth. Bob spoke first, "I'm leaving Ford Motors, Kegham. I'm going..." Kegham's aroused, angry voice cut in, "What happened, Bob?! Tell me!"

"Calm down ol' buddy. It's not what you think. I'm going to start my own law firm with two of my Harvard classmates. Union contracts and labor laws are complicating the work place. My experience will go a long way. We've already found office space in New York City."

Kegham's face mirrored traces of abandonment and disappointment. Bob sensed it and turned the direction of the conversation. "Well, isn't my brother going to wish me success?" purposely couching his voice with a touch of regret.

Kegham quickly responded. He reached across the table, grabbing Bob's shoulders in a firm grip, and poured out an avalanche of well-wishes. The corner booth came alive with excitement. A few customers glanced at the direction of the commotion and continued eating.

69

New Directions

The last Friday of the month was Parent-Teacher Conference Night at Hally Elementary School. The old grading system—1-excellent, 2-good, 3-fair, 4-poor, 5-failure—was replaced with "E-excellent, S-satisfactory, and U-unsatisfactory," with additional spaces to check a student's behavior for courtesy, study habits, promptness, cooperation, self-control, and other attributes. Both parents wanted to find out the reason for the three check marks in the self-control column, so a silent Martin walked with his parents to school for some answers.

Miss Short, his arithmetic teacher, gave the same accounting as the other teachers, "He's always waving his hand, trying to get attention to the exclusion of the rest of the class." Miss Short humorously added, "It's a good thing Martin's desk is in the last row or else he'd have his hand right in my face." She continued, "There are times when his energy and enthusiasm get the best of him. He runs down the aisle, pleading, 'Miss Short! Miss Short'...." She couldn't help laughing—"At least he doesn't shout out the answers."

Kegham silently thought to himself, "At least there's some self-control."

Both parents promised to help curb Martin's bursts of enthusiasm. All in all, it was a good conference.

Walking home in the cool evening air felt refreshing. Mother and son leisurely walked a few steps ahead of Kegham, who enjoyed observing his family. It gave him great inner joy and deep satisfaction listening to their conversations.

Halfway home, Martin's exuberance broke loose. "Mom, could you bake a pineapple upside down cake for Miss Short? Please?" The request was obvious—student diplomacy in all its transparency.

Hazel countered, "That doesn't change the fact that you have to work on your self-control in school."

An impatient response, "I know, Mom, I know."

On the way home, they passed Sanders Cleaners main plant and Kegham's eye caught a notice in the corner of the large plate-glass window, "Interviewing for Plant Manager." A couple of thoughts crossed his mind: "So close to home" and "Bob's in New York...."

At home, the persistent diplomat continued pressing his request. Hazel agreed, "Remember, the cake is to be shared with the whole class."

Martin had his own plan. Later in school, he added a note, "Dear Miss Short, This cake is for you.

You don't have to share it with the class. I promise to have more self-control. Your friend, Martin." It was an innocent expression of a child's affection for his teacher.

Sanders had become Detroit's largest dry-cleaning business, owned by the Olson family for two generations. By 1934, it had grown to 60 stores. A fleet of trucks picked up the clothes and took them to the main plant, where they were dry-cleaned, pressed, bagged, and returned to their respective stores.

Fred Olson, Sr. was still active in the management of the day-to-day operations. His father had come to America from Sweden in the 1850s, settling in one of the small Minnesota farming communities.

Saturday morning, after a quick cup of coffee, a few hurried bites of *kata* a la Turfanda, and Kegham was off to the Sanders plant. He introduced himself to the store clerk. "It just so happens, Mr. A…lg..n, that Mr. Olson Sr. is in this morning. He's usually never here on Saturdays. Please wait, Mr. Ag..l..n.." Kegham helped the clerk on the pronunciation. "I'll just be a minute," and disappeared behind the drape covering the opening leading into the plant.

Kegham was led up a narrow steel staircase to a small austere room with a desk and two chairs. The room had a bird's-eye view of the sprawling plant below. A stout, white-haired, pink-cheeked man in his

80's greeted him with a smile and a warm friendly handshake that immediately put Kegham at ease.

Strange thoughts were starting to crowd his mind, "What am I doing here? I already have a job!" But something was happening. Events were unfolding and he was responding.

Mr. Olson never stopped smiling, "What is your experience in the dry-cleaning business— especially in the managerial end of the business?" Kegham began, explaining his dry-cleaning venture, and his position at Ford Motor Company. He was starting to go into more detail, but Mr. Olson politely interrupted, "Excuse me, Mr. Agegian..."—Kegham was impressed, the right pronunciation the first time— "...did you serve during the Great War?"

"Yes, sir. I was in the field artillery." A short pause followed that lasted long enough to mean "please continue."

Kegham related some of his experiences while training, and about his comrades. "Did you have any close encounters with the enemy?" interrupted Mr. Olson. He was definitely more interested in war experiences than the details of army life.

Kegham paused to begin again, when the words, "Can you use another SOB?" popped into his head.

"We had one great commanding officer, Colonel Halverson. He..."

"Did you say Halverson?!"

"Bjorn Halverson!!"

Mr. Olson was invigorated with delight, "Your Colonel is my first cousin; our mothers were sisters." For all intents and purposes, the interview had just ended. "I'll match Ford's salary and add a Christmas bonus."

Kegham sat nonplussed, staring at Mr. Olson's extended hand. It all happened so fast—"Have I just been hired?"

Mr. Olson helped relieve some of the pressure. 'Of course you need to discuss this with your family." They walked down the stairs together, and shook hands again. Kegham thanked the nice lady behind the counter and headed for home, a little bewildered but somewhat content.

A salary equal to Ford's plus a Christmas bonus and only 15 minutes' walk from home. He tried to visualize a smiling Hazel as he headed for home. It somehow didn't materialize.

After dinner, Martin went out to be with his friends. In an hour, the street lights would flicker on, signaling the children that it was time to wind up last bits of conversation and head for home.

Hazel cleared the table, "Where did you go this morning in such a hurry? You skipped your usual scrambled eggs and tomatoes." A hesitant response, "I went…to the Sanders plant."

Hazel had also noticed the sign in the window, the night before. Kegham began to list the litany of reasons for changing jobs: the round-trip travel time, three hours versus thirty minutes, equal salary plus bonus, clothes dry-cleaned free of charge, family owned business—not another number on the time card…. The biggest hurdle was the company car. He struggled to make favorable additions to the list of reasons. Hazel turned. She was smiling, "There's always public transportation."

A stunned Kegham blurted, "It shouldn't be too hard to find a good used car."

From the upstairs front porch, Kegham's familiar long, shrill, two-finger whistle pierced the evening air. From the street below came a youthful voice, "Coming, Dad."

Detroit was in the grip of an unusually cold January. Snow had been steadily falling since early morning. In Miss Short's class, the children were on the edge of their seats waiting for the last click on the wall clock. Martin crouched like a runner poised for the 100-yard dash. The bell sent its message. The room started to empty—"Bye, Miss Short," was greeted with a loving smile until her last student rushed by. Then came that moment of melancholy — the silent, empty classroom. Miss Short picked up their homework papers, her purse, and consoled herself, "But my darlings will be back tomorrow."

It was an ideal day for building a snowman and snowball fights. As Martin ran up the stairs, he heard voices. His mother had invited several of her lady friends for an afternoon tea party. After greeting everyone, he rushed to his bedroom to change into after-school clothes. His bed was covered with coats and, next to each coat, one, two...six purses. As he continued undressing, his eyes never left the purses.

Fully dressed—but a force was preventing him from rushing outside—other thoughts were already crowding out the snowman and snowball fights. He hung up his school clothes. Like an invisible magnet, the purses were drawing his attention. A reaction to an unfolding was about to happen.

Then, in an agonizing, guilt-ridden moment, Martin nervously removed ten cents from each purse. It was an attempt at fairness, a novel concept when stealing.

Sixty cents meant six model airplane kits. Martin ran through the heavy snowfall until he reached the hobby store. There was no trouble deciding what the young customer wanted. The store clerk waited and listened. "I want the SE5 Scout, Fokker D7, Spad, Sopwith Camel, Nieuport, and Fokker Tri-plane— Baron Manfred von Richthofen's red triplane was the terror of the skies during the first war. The "Red

Baron" was credited with downing 80 airplanes before going to his death.

The guests had already gone; his dad was still at work and his mom was in the kitchen preparing dinner. Martin slipped into his room and put the boxes under his bed. "It wasn't stealing a lot—after all, what's one dime out of a purse full of coins." The rationale made sense as conscience took a back seat.

Martin gulped down his dinner and was off to his room. Ten minutes later, Kegham, on the way to the bathroom, noticed Martin's closed door. Martin never closed his bedroom door. Curiosity got the best of him and he peeked in. Martin was sitting at his work table in deep concentration, cutting out the printed parts from a sheet of balsa wood.

His father's presence in the doorway was unexpected. Martin's surprised look indicated something was just not right.

Kegham's eyes caught a glimpse of the boxes under the bed. Martin sat motionless. The question was straight forward, "Where did you get the money, Martin?"

The reply was quick, "I found it, Dad." The answer reeked with suspicion.

Gulps of saliva and a blank look called for further questioning. "How much did you find?" The interrogation was getting unbearable.

"Six dimes," was the answer. The suspect couldn't go on, "I took them from the purses on my bed. I only took one dime and no more, honest, Dad." A torrent of tears followed the confession.

The hurt on his parents' faces and the lecture that followed was unbearable. Martin solemnly followed his father down the seemingly never-ending back stairs to the basement, straight to the furnace. His father opened the furnace door and stepped back. There was no doubt as to what had to be done. The flames devoured each box as Martin threw them in, one by one. Last was the partially assembled Fokker Triplane wrapped in its plans. Baron von Richthofen's triplane went to a fiery end for a repeat performance, this time in the basement furnace at 15790 - 14th Street and not in the skies over France.

Fred Olson, Sr.'s, admiration for his loyal and dedicated plant manager grew through the years that followed. Many times Mr. Olson would watch from his office trying to find the key to Kegham's ability to combine managerial responsibilities with touches of friendship with so many employees. What he would never know was how the years of the unfolding of events had shaped his plant manager's character and personality.

The First World War was heralded as "the war to end all wars." In time, the sustaining power of the idea was lost. It became just another emotionally charged phrase. Twenty years later, in 1939, Europe was again at war over the very same roads in swift tanks, through the same cities with an added attraction—deadly aerial bombing reduced whole city blocks into mangled steel and shattered concrete. Civilians became legitimate targets this time.

Americans saw on the movie screen and read about the beleaguered French and British forces fighting a losing battle against a powerful German army whose *blitzkrieg* ("lightening war") tactics raced through Belgium and France in six weeks, forcing the British Expeditionary Forces at Dunkirk to barely escape total annihilation. Only through the heroic efforts of the Royal Navy, private yachts, fishing boats and even rowboats evacuating the retreating army were they rescued. It was one of the lowest points of the war for the Allies.

President Roosevelt's popularity could not change America's neutrality policy—Americans were not going to shed American blood for a second time in a European war.

American companies were content to do business with both sides. It was all about profits. Busy plants meant less unemployment at a time when the US economy still hadn't freed itself from the grip of the "Great Depression."

However, Sunday morning, December 7, 1941, it all changed. The unprovoked attack on the US Pacific Naval Base at Pearl Harbor, Hawaii, by the carrier-based aircraft of the Imperial Japanese Navy changed America's isolationist position overnight.

On December 8th, President Roosevelt, leaning on the speaker's dais in heavy steel leg braces—a result of polio—asked Congress for a declaration of war between the United States and the Japanese Empire for what he called, "a dastardly act…that will live in infamy."

The roar of approval filled the great chamber. Isolationists, like the dinosaurs, suddenly vanished. It was time again for patriotic songs, speeches, and war bonds.

Unemployment figures began dropping. America was to become "the arsenal of democracy," ready to continue to fulfill its "assignment of Destiny."

In January 1942, Martin was in the 12th grade at Cooley High School. Kegham was in his fourth year at Sanders Cleaners. Fred Olson's respect and friendship never wavered and steadily grew, as did the Christmas bonuses.

Kegham drove his old battered Pontiac to the dealership—signed the necessary papers and drove out of the show room in a new 1942 Plymouth sedan—the last year Detroit's "Big Three" manufacturers would produce cars for public sale until 1946. It was his first new car. The new-car smell was tantalizing. Life at 15790 - 14th Street was never better. He quietly evoked his personal mantra, "God bless Amerika."

70

Amerika – "I Love You"

Something was bothering Kegham. The moments of contemplation were becoming more frequent. Hazel's instincts became alerted; she was determined to find the reason.

America was at war and hidden deep inside Kegham's psyche was the young immigrant yearning to help the country he had come to love. Kegham pondered, "Hazel will have to understand why I must leave Sanders and work in a war defense plant."

The lyrics of a World War I song summed up his feelings; now if he could only sing it to Hazel. The idea was farfetched. He tried singing it one night walking home from work,

"America, I love you. You're like a sweetheart of mine.

From ocean to ocean, you're my devotion touching each boundary line.

Just like a little baby climbing its mother's knee

America, I love you and there's a hundred million others like me."

The years of warm, congenial relationship with Fred Olson Sr. weighed heavily on Kegham. Being ungrateful was not one of his character traits.

Sanders offered many possibilities. Fred Olson Jr. showed little interest in running the family business. His father was relying more and more on Kegham.

Hazel had often said, "You could be a part-owner someday."

Right after dinner, Martin went to his bedroom to finish an algebra assignment. The quiet was suddenly shattered by his mother's piercing loud voice, "YOU WANT TO LEAVE SANDERS?!???"

Martin decided to stay in his room and listen. "Kegham, have you lost your senses. You have a secure job working for a wonderful employer. Something has happened that you're not telling me." Hazel wasn't smiling. The financial future of the family was at stake—"You can forget the patriotic song, Kegham."

Kegham's faltering voice responded, "Nothing has happened at the plant...I...I..." Hazel's patience had already evaporated.

An aggravated wife listened to her husband's reasons for his decision to leave. She tried every tactic and argument against leaving Sanders. This was their first serious confrontation. Several times, Hazel caught herself in the high-decibel range and lowered her voice so as not to alarm the Nersessians downstairs. After an hour of heated discussion, it came to an abrupt end. An ominous quiet settled in the kitchen. Martin strained his ears. Hazel's instincts told her it was useless to continue. Her husband was not going to change his mind.

Her strategy shifted, "You're definitely not going to work as an ordinary laborer on some dirty, oily machine stamping out parts."

Kegham drew a deep breath. The only problem now was how to say "good-bye" to Mr. Olson.

Skilled workers were at a premium in war-time America. Hazel meticulously scanned the *Detroit News* want-ad section every day. Her quest ended. The Lawrence Institute of Technology was offering a two-month intensive course for precision inspector certification. Course requirements: knowledge of the decimal system and the ability to read blueprints. Classes were to start in two weeks. Kegham rushed to enroll.

"Martin, you're going to help your dad for the next two weeks and teach him all you know about blueprints, the decimal system, and …" Hazel handed her son the requirements of the course.

A jubilant Kegham was all smiles, "I'm ready, teacher, but don't forget I'm still your dad."

Hazel quickly added, "Don't forget who's the principal!"

For the next two weeks, father and son worked on the decimal system, how to measure and read a caliper, micrometer, and other delicate measuring devices, plus reading and interpreting a wide range of blueprints that Martin brought home from school, thanks to his metal shop teacher who generously cooperated.

Class started after dinner and continued into the night. Martin was amazed how quickly his dad learned. The principal listened attentively from the living room to the teacher/student chatter in the kitchen.

Kegham stood facing Mr. Olson sitting behind his desk. "Is the plant shut down for the night?"

"Yes, sir, all shut and locked tight," which meant the giant steam oil furnace control setting was in the "off" position, all overhead doors down, and windows locked. That day's finished garments were in their appropriate racks ready for tomorrow's delivery trucks.

Kegham painfully began to explain his decision to leave. Mr. Olson slumped in his chair in a saddened state of shock. No matter how caringly and with every ounce of sincerity Kegham endeavored to show the gratitude and respect he had for Mr. Olson, somehow it fell short of accomplishing its purpose. A deeply hurt Mr. Olson couldn't hide his feelings that spoke through his eyes.

Any attempt to counter Kegham's reasons for leaving were abandoned. Both men were emotionally affected. Mr. Olson, with great effort, said, "My best to you, Kegham." They shook hands. There was no need for a two-week notice.

A sad and pensive Kegham left Sanders for the last time. He sat at the kitchen table, a lonely figure. Hazel joined him. She pondered, "I should not have given up so easily," thus generating a feeling of guilt, which she bore silently.

A confident, smiling Martin strutted across Cooley High School auditorium stage waving his diploma at his parents somewhere in the audience. For Kegham, it was a time of pride and remembrance of the events of his life's journey that led to this moment of sublime serenity millions of miles from Khunoos.

Some graduates had already paid their visit to the recruiting officer. Others were content to wait for their draft notices. Both parents shared inescapable anxieties about the future of their only child, the very core of their existence.

Homes on 14th Street were beginning to display the white and red banner with a blue star in their living room windows in remembrance of a family member serving in the armed forces.

A gold star meant that the ultimate sacrifice had been made. It never failed to leave a sobering effect on those passing by.

Kegham confidently continued his classes at Lawrence Tech. Martin was ready to help his dad on difficult problems. Kegham passed the final exam and walked out of school a successful graduate holding an official looking certificate.

In celebration, the principal baked a pineapple upside-down cake in honor of the graduate and his teacher. They sat around the kitchen table, talking, eating, and laughing.

Martin scoured every inch of the *Detroit News* for the notice announcing air cadet exams. According to the recruiting officer, tests were scheduled for some time in February.

Hazel found the *one*-column, three-inch announcement: "US Army Air Cadet Examinations will be held on Thursday, February 10, at 450 East Jefferson Avenue at 9 a.m."

She carefully cut out the notice and placed it in the side drawer of her sewing machine. After a long pause, she took it out and re-read the words of the announcement and placed it back into the drawer.

Hazel waited until the family was together for dinner. "Martin, I think this is what you've been looking for." A jubilant Martin hugged his mother. An uneasy feeling settled over Hazel. Kegham didn't know how to react. There was no way to delay the inevitable. Their only child was going to war.

Martin joined the long line of eager applicants impatiently pushing against each other. The door opened exactly at 9:00 a.m. A spacious room with chairs behind long rows of tables rapidly filled. The overflow of applicants were told to return for the 1:00 p.m. test. The line held fast—no one moved.

A staff sergeant, vintage of the last war, gave the prepared, short explanation about the test. Four privates passed out the test booklets and pencils. "Do not open the test book. You have two hours to complete the exam. When finished, place it in this box. You are then free to leave. A letter of acceptance to the Flight Cadet Program will arrive in about ten days." There was a short pause as the sergeant's eyes looked across the room making sure everyone understood.

The sergeant looked at his stop watch while the hopefuls waited with pencils poised. "Begin." The test book covers flew back as each applicant withdrew in a world of his own. The silence was broken only by the sounds of turning pages. The US Army Air Force was in the initial phase of selecting the best candidates. Those who survived the next 10 months of rigid disciplined training would be the Class of February 1944 (44B).

The sergeant watched from his desk like a prison guard looking for irregularities in the conduct of the inmates. "Time's up!" The room was already half empty. The "geniuses" had finished before the two-hour deadline. Martin took the full two hours going over each question a second and third time.

Hazel was home alone when she took the official looking envelope out of the mailbox. She knew its contents were going to change the course of her son's life. She was slightly bewildered as to why she was so excited. The letter was propped against the vase on the dining room table so it faced the door. Both parents were in the kitchen, waiting. The sounds of bounding footsteps up the stairs. A moment of silence. "I passed! I passed!" The outburst rolled on like thunder filling the dining room and spilling into the kitchen. All through dinner, his parents listened to their ecstatic son. They sat alone, staring at each other, while Martin gobbled down his dinner and rushed to break the news to his friend, Roy Sahakian.

Martin and Roy lived in adjacent upstairs flats. Every morning before going to school, they would talk to each other from their bathroom windows about 10 feet away. Roy was a disparagingly quiet boy. He reveled in Martin's extroverted and engaging personality. They were a perfect match. Martin led, and Roy followed.

Martin left for flight training a month before Roy was drafted into the Army. "Roy, do me a favor—get a desk job. You can type 60 words a minute and even can take shorthand." (Roy had followed commercial courses at Cooley High.) Martin was trying to protect his friend.

"I promise, Martin."

"Now you're talking, Roy."

Three months later, Hazel forwarded a letter from Roy to Thunderbird Field, Arizona, where Martin had just started primary flight school—many in the class of 44B never got beyond primary school. Martin eagerly opened the letter postmarked Fort Hood, Texas.

"Hi Martin…You know how I've always been shy and awkward—I know what I promised when we last saw each other. As you can see, I've joined the Tank Destroyer Corps (TD)….Your pal, Roy."

Roy landed in Normandy D-Day plus three, and never stopped fighting until May 6, 1945. He saw enough action and close calls for a platoon of marines. He returned from the war the same shy, gentle young man. Nothing had changed except for a more mature bearing. Roy went on to become the head of one of Ford Motor's accounting departments. Martin was best man at his wedding.

US Industry became the primary source of war material for America's chief allies—England and the Soviet Union. Skilled labor held the highest priority in the general work force and was highly sought after.

Hazel sat at the kitchen table studying the want ad sections of the *Detroit News*. Several ads were checked. A host of small companies had sprouted all around Detroit as a result of the war.

"I'm going out for a while—do you need anything for tonight's dinner?"

"Yes, get about two pounds of okra and one pound of lean lamb." He could almost taste his favorite—okra lamb stew and rice pilaf. He picked up the ration book on the way out.

Kegham had decided earlier to pay a visit to Lawrence Tech to see his instructor, Mr. Fuller. "Maybe he could give me some leads for jobs." It was just a thought, but it merited investigation.

Mr. Fuller greeted him with an enthusiastic handshake. Before Kegham could explain his reason for coming, Mr. Fuller started, "Mr. Agegian, your visit could not have been timed any better. I just finished talking to Mr. Ormanski at Packard Motors. He's looking for a precision inspector, and you're just the man for the job."

"It sounds great, Mr. Fuller," was his eager reply. Mr. Fuller immediately phoned Mr. Ormanski, and in a few minutes, an appointment for 2:30 that afternoon was scheduled.

"Go to gate 4B. He'll be expecting you." Kegham thanked Mr. Fuller and headed for the Royal Market to do the shopping.

Hazel plugged in the iron. In minutes, she was ironing out the wrinkles in Kegham's suit. "Your white shirt is in the closet and bring your favorite red tie, your black dress shoes—they're in the Tom McCann shoe box on the top shelf of our closet."

The possibility of a new job generates its own kind of excitement. Hazel carefully inspected the applicant. "Now that's the way a precision inspector should go for a job interview." The kitchen clock was approaching 1:30, plenty of time for the 2:30 appointment.

The timing was near perfect. At gate 4B, he asked for Mr. Ormanski. A large, powerful-looking man greeted him. "I understand you're a Lawrence Tech graduate."

"Yes, I attended a two-month intensive, precision inspector's program," Kegham handed him his inspector's credentials. The department head studied it briefly.

For the next hour, Mr. Ormanski explained the depth and breadth of the position. "Aircraft engine parts require precise and exacting inspection—there's a great deal of responsibility resting on an inspector's shoulders...."

Kegham listened with heightened interest. By 3:30, the interview was over. He filled out his application. "Mr. Agegian, as far as I'm concerned, you're the right man for the job—but the final word has to come from the FBI. They need to make a background check on all inspectors. It's a precaution against possible saboteurs and '5th column agents.'

The report takes about four days." He thought for a few seconds, "If all goes well, you'll begin work next Monday. How's that sound?"

"Sounds great, sir." They walked to the gate, shook hands, and parted.

What a day! "Thanks, Lawrence Tech—thanks, Mr. Fuller—thanks, Mr. Ormanski—thanks, Hazel." The tempting smell of okra lamb stew was playing havoc with his taste buds.

God Bless Amerika!

71

The FBI

Kegham answered the phone—Mr. Ormanski's call was to the point. "You cleared the FBI background check with flying colors. I'll see you Monday. Congratulations."

Kegham's "Thanks" came a second too late— no doubt he was busy with pressing matters. "Hazel, I'm starting Monday!" Hazel's eyes lit up; her pride for her husband wasn't about to be concealed.

Mr. Ormanski introduced Kegham to a tall, slender man in his 60s. "Meet Joe Mitchell, our lead inspector. Joe wrote the book on precision inspecting. You'll be in good hands." The department head placed a friendly pat on Kegham's shoulder and left.

"How do you pronounce your name?" Kegham pronounced each syllable slowly. Bingo! Joe was right on target and never had to be corrected.

Joe Mitchell methodically explained the work of the inspecting department. His meticulous, detailed description of every step of the inspection process belied his years of experience.

Packard Motors was licensed in early 1941 to build Rolls-Royce Merlin engines for the famous Hurricane and Spitfire fighter planes of the RAF. "It's like a giant Swiss watch—every part has to be made to exacting measurements with little tolerances." They continued down the line, while Joe Mitchell explained in detail the various parts and where they fit into the powerful 1520 hp liquid-cooled engine.

"We've started fitting our P-51 Mustangs with Merlin's..."

Kegham proudly interrupted, "My son, Martin, is in the Air Force Cadet program. He's already soloed."

Joe responded, "Maybe he'll fly a P-51." The implications didn't escape Kegham, it only strengthened his belief that everything that had taken place in his life was due to the guiding hand of his personal destiny.

Joe detracted Kegham's thoughts, "Tomorrow you'll start inspecting propeller shaft components. I've got a few more things to go over with you before you start wielding your micrometer."

With each passing week, Kegham's reputation as a flawless inspector grew to such a degree that Mr. Ormanski submitted his name to the War Production Board's Award for Excellence.

Kegham's initials, KA, were respected for their flawless accuracy by the machine operators. In one month, the number of rejections dropped dramatically. His gentle manner won the confidence of his co-workers who exerted their best to be near perfect.

The mass production lines required a trial run, and parts were randomly inspected. If they passed Kegham's close scrutiny, the go-ahead was given and the green tag initialed KA would be set aside with the inspected part, as proof of his acceptance.

One day, while heading for his locker at the end of the shift, Joe was waiting. Joe's expression was sober and serious. "Kegham—Mr. Ormanski wants to see us."

As soon as they entered, the department head began, "Mr. Agegian, I want you to meet agents Bracken and Randall from the FBI." The agents were already sizing up their suspect.

Agent Randall started, "Are these your initials on these green tags?" "Yes, they are, but I didn't write them."

"Please write your initials five times."

It was plain to everyone that they didn't match. A welcomed sense of relief came over Mr. Ormanski. "What's our next step, gentlemen?"

Agent Bracken laid out a simple plan. Starting tomorrow, two FBI agents would be disguised as floor sweepers on Mr. Agegian's shift. Nothing was going to escape their scrutiny. The meeting ended.

On the second day, one of the sweeper agents caught the man forging Kegham's initials on a defective part. It turned out to be a case of jealousy and prejudice, not sabotage.

A month later, following a short informal presentation in Mr. Ormanski's office, Kegham walked back into the plant with the glass-framed Certificate of Excellence. His fellow workers cheered and applauded. He held up the award, "Thanks, but the award belongs to all of us," and looked for a place to hang it.

72

Officer and Gentleman

Fifteen hundred miles away, the 100 members of the class of 44B at the advanced twin engine school in Marfa, Texas, stood at attention on the tarmac waiting for the graduation ceremonies to end.

No longer cadets! The 2nd lieutenant gold bars and the silver wings completed their tailored officers' uniforms. Three weeks before graduation, a uniform contracting firm from Kansas City had sent several tailors to take individual measurements. There would be no baggy pants, loose-fitting jackets, or billowing shirts for the new crop of "officers and gentlemen." Nineteen-year-old Martin joined the spontaneous cheers for the ten-day leave.

Both parents strained their eyes for a glimpse of their son. Grandparents sat on a bench patiently waiting. Michigan Central Station was an undulating blend of military uniforms and civilian clothes.

The irony of the moment was painfully evident to Kegham—another war—this time it was called World War Two.

"I see him! Martin! Martin!" Hazel's voice was electrifying. The light of their eyes rushed towards his family joyously waving and shouting. The "officer and gentleman" was lost in the moment of youthful exuberance of a boy coming home.

The ten days evaporated without mercy, the victim of a whirlwind of dinner invitations. Not to be left out was a special visit to Hally Elementary School.

Martin stood in the open doorway of Miss Short's room. She turned to leave with an armful of homework to correct, "Martin!" She couldn't get out of her chair. Her impetuous student rushed in and placed a large tray on her desk, hugged his favorite teacher, and headed to his desk in the last row. "Miss Short! Miss Short!" Martin rushed up the aisle waving his hands. They couldn't stop laughing.

For the next hour, Miss Short sat spell-bound, listening to the same energized 5th grader whom she had given a checkmark for self-control. A tearful Miss Short hugged Martin, knowing that another student was about to join the plethora of memories whose names and faces would fade away with the passing of time.

For Martin, the carefree joys of childhood memories were also slipping away. The empty classroom's eerie silence enveloped Miss Short as she read the note left with the pineapple upside down cake—"Dear Miss Short, this cake is for you. You don't have to share it with anyone. To my favorite teacher, Martin." Tears trickled down her cheeks blurring the words "favorite teacher."

On the ninth day, father and son went to Packard Motors. Mr. Ormanski greeted Martin. "Congratulations on those silver wings, young man."

"It's been my dream to be a pilot since I was a kid," answered Martin.

"Mr. Agegian, take your son for a tour of the department. Your dad is Packard's top inspector." Martin gave his father a strong, one-arm hug. Kegham looked up at his son's face. There wasn't a meter capable of measuring the love between a father and son.

As they made the rounds between aisles of lathes, milling machines, and presses, it became clear to Martin that the smiles and friendly greetings were for the "top inspector"—the gentle, soft-spoken man he had the honor to call "Dad."

That evening, dinner at Grandma's was followed by card games that Martin had been part of since he was eight years old.

The unspoken words and hidden emotions were silently taking their toll on the family. For Second Lieutenant Agegian, it was on to B-17 transition school and then to meet the other nine members of his crew. The flak-filled skies over France and Germany were a few months away. This time it wasn't model airplanes in mock battle positions hanging from his bedroom ceiling, but real live diving Messerschmitt 109s spitting death at formations of B-17 Flying Fortresses.

"*Der Arvadz* (Lord God), watch over my Martin," was Turfanda's nightly reminder to God up to the day she peacefully passed away in her sleep in February 1945. Grandpa Krikor—tough, stubborn—ripped off heels and soles with a vengeance, cursing the world.

Kegham and Hazel anxiously waited for each tissue-thin V-mail letter from their son. The once vaunted invincible armed forces of the Third Reich officially surrendered on May 8, 1945. Victory in Europe, VE Day, was officially declared. Hitler took the easy way out and shoved a pistol barrel into his mouth and blew his tonsils out the back of his head. Eva Braun, his bride of two days, took poison. Both bodies were soaked in gasoline and burned beyond recognition.

The 34th Bomber group began preparations to leave. Martin's crew and 10 additional ground crew personnel tried to make themselves comfortable inside the B-17. The bomb bay was covered with plywood to hold all their personal belongings, souvenirs—and a few cases of beer for celebrating at 8,000 feet.

They left their base on June 21, 1945, six days before Martin's 21st birthday. Their route took them to Greenland, Goose Bay, Labrador, and finally to Bradley Field, Connecticut. The field was a mass of B-17's. Martin cut the four engines off for the last time. He placed the delivery receipt for the B-17 in his flight jacket, and joined the crew to celebrate that night before leaving on a ten-day leave.

So much had changed from the day ten years ago when Martin had stood in front of the furnace throwing his ill-gotten model airplanes into the fire.

The family was in tears as they hugged the light of their lives. Grandpa was noticeably bent over and Martin's parents looked so much older—it had to be the streaks of premature grey hair.

There still was an enemy to defeat in the Pacific. Next stop: Roswell, New Mexico, and B-29 transition school and a new crew. On August 6th, the first atomic bomb devastated Hiroshima. The awesome, billowing mushroom cloud of smoke rose miles into the clear blue sky. One B-29 had delivered the devastating bomb. Americans held their breath—as did the US military. Japan was not forthcoming with overtures of surrender. On August 9th, the second atomic bomb scorched and radiated thousands of bodies and buildings in Nagasaki. There was only one option left for Japan.

On the battleship *USS Missouri* in Tokyo Bay, his Imperial Majesty Emperor Hirohito's representatives, standing stiff and sullen, faced a small table surrounded by the victors.

US General Douglas MacArthur, Supreme Commander of the Pacific Theatre of Operations, motioned to the representatives to sign the unconditional surrender terms.

V-J Day joined V-E Day. Six years of war and millions of deaths and casualties finally came to an end. In many families, fathers and sons had fought in two world wars. Was this to be the war to end all wars?

73

The Final Unfolding

For the 12 million returning service men and women, their grateful government offered a unique opportunity—the GI Bill of Rights. Besides generous terms for home loans and business start-up loans, it provided one very important provision that allowed veterans to enroll in universities, colleges, and trade schools with tuition picked up by Uncle Sam, plus a $75-a-month stipend. Young Americans streamed into the campuses. America eagerly took the road to normalcy, full of optimism, while the rest of the world wearily faced the grim task of rebuilding destroyed cities, disrupted social structures, and shattered lives.

Former enemies, Germany and Japan, became the recipients of America's generosity—the hand of friendship from a forgiving victor reached across the Atlantic and Pacific with food and capital goods.

Martin graduated with a BA from Wayne University majoring in European history. His ambition was to follow in the footsteps of the legendary American journalist, Edward R. Murrow.

After graduating in 1949, he worked on several newspapers—*Detroit News, Wyandotte Tribune, Associated Press*—five years in northern Ontario, Canada managing a logging operation—back to Detroit and a series of jobs of short duration. He couldn't settle down—a problem that plagued many veterans.

Then something happened. It was the image of an excited Miss Short rushing down the aisle, shouting "Martin, Martin!" A sudden decision and back to Wayne University for his teaching credential. He began teaching in Livonia, a suburb of Detroit, where he eventually met his future wife, Cessy.

Kegham and Hazel continued living out their lives. Just before their 47th wedding anniversary, Hazel succumbed to liver cancer. The beautiful young girl Kegham first saw that fateful night in the hall above the Woolworth Store was no longer to be a part of his life.

He sold their home and moved to an apartment complex. Martin and his wife had moved to California a few years before his mother's death. Kegham made trips to California and Martin to Michigan. Kegham's visits never lasted more than a week. "Dad, you practically just arrived and now you're leaving?" The reason was simple; the pinochle games, backgammon boards, and reminiscing with old friends filled a need that only he could explain.

Life was gradually slowing down for Kegham. His secretive nature never let anyone know the condition of his health. "I feel just fine—just getting older," was the stock answer. His legs were weakening and painful when standing too long.

Reoccurring chest pains were ignored as a passing phenomenon.

"This is my last game boys. I'm going for an early start for home before the snow starts causing traffic problems." Saint John's Senior Men's Club membership totaled about 75 men--like Kegham, many were orphaned during the genocide. The muffled sounds of their voices faded away behind the closed door of the clubroom. Pulling out of the parking lot, he recalled an eager young man many years ago learning to drive. It was a short drive to the apartment. The heavy snowfall slowed down traffic—it didn't matter.

Kegham slowly climbed the stairs, pausing at the landing to catch his breath. The warmth of his apartment felt good. He laid his coat on the arm chair and went straight to his bedroom—"I'll warm up dinner later." He sat on the edge of the bed, visibly fatigued and perspiring. The row of family photos on the dresser stood like silent witnesses. Kegham laid down on his bed and looked up at the ceiling. His eyes focused on its smooth surface—staring, seeking, and searching for traces of past joys and memories. The sliver of light separating life from death was fading. Eternity was just a few breaths away.

His final words blended into the silence....

"God Bless.....AH-MER-I-KA"